To Hal -
Friends mean everything.
Warmest regards.
Amy Montgomery
3-16-05

Just an Accident

by

Amy Montgomery

Doctors and therapists brought Scott Remington
back from the brink.
Regular folks brought him back to life... twice.

authorHOUSE™

1663 LIBERTY DRIVE, SUITE 200
BLOOMINGTON, INDIANA 47403
(800) 839-8640
WWW.AUTHORHOUSE.COM

First published by AuthorHouse 12/30/04

ISBN: 1-4184-9290-6 (sc)

Library of Congress Control Number: 2004111482

Printed in the United States of America
Bloomington, Indiana

This book is printed on acid-free paper.

Cover design: Marilyn Jones

To Charlie

For opening my eyes to a new possibility
and for the freedom to run with it.

The family

<u>Scott's parents</u>
John "Bull" - father
Gertrude - mother

<u>Scott's children</u>
John "Roscoe" and Jenna

<u>Scott's siblings</u>
Earle - brother

Denise MacGlashan - sister
Bill MacGlashan - Denise's husband
Miranda, Christopher, Jeffrey, and Jeremy - Denise and Bill's children

Stephanie Wood - sister
Keith Wood - Steph's husband
Adrian and Dakota - Steph and Keith's children

Renee Smith - sister
John Smith - Renee's husband
Joss-Elyse - Renee and John's daughter

Contents

Introduction xi

Part I 1

    1.   Gearing Up Again. 5
    2.   "A widow maker, so they call 'em". 18
    3.   The troop mobilization 31
    4.   The "after" begins. 42
    5.   A vigil tied in blue. 55
    6.   Sealed with a KISS 63
    7.   A squeeze and a wink. 74
    8.   A man *of* the woods 99

Part II 115

    9.   You can't make this up 119
    10. Home sweet unknown. 159
    11. From all outward appearances 173
    12. ... do us part 189
    13. Like the tree that hit him 210

Part III. 225

    14. Change of heart (and mind) 229
    15. High and way inside. 254
    16. Onward. 271

Afterthoughts. 282

Note of Thanks 287

Introduction

The weirdest part is that there wasn't a mark on him, not a bruise, no black and blue marks, no cuts or scrapes, not a drop of blood.

But when the top of a massive beech tree snapped off unexpectedly and smacked into thirty-three-year-old logger Scott Remington—who was standing on the ground at that moment securing a bunch of freshly-cut trees to his skidder cable—it crushed his insides. "I was tying up the last tree of that hitch," says Scott, shaking his head from the irony of it all. "Everything was all cut, and I was just hooking them up."

The treetop hit him in the back, and Scott guesses that he lunged forward, hit the downed tree that he was tying, and was thrown back by the impact. His older brother, Earle, would eventually find Scott lying face-up in the woods beside his chainsaw and skidder, whose motor was still running, with that huge piece of beech cradling his neck like a pillow. Earle thinks that when Scott felt the impact of the tree, "He musta fought it back." No one will ever really know what happened in that split second of impact, but one thing's for sure, says Earle, "Scott's pretty strong."

So was that treetop. Beech is a particularly dense and heavy wood, and this was a section maybe twenty-five, thirty feet long and almost fourteen inches in diameter. An ice storm the previous winter probably weighted the treetop until it partially snapped, hanging by one live thread "way up in the canopy," says Scott, waiting for something or someone to finish the job. "Whether I dislodged it when I felled another tree near it or the wind blew," he says, "I don't know."

No telling how long Scott lay there before his father, John, got worried and sent Earle to have a look-see. Father and sons, all loggers, were working a job deep in the woods up near Blue Ridge, New York—sixty to seventy miles from the Canadian border and about twenty miles north of the Remingtons' hometown of Brant Lake. John was stationed on the gravel logging road, waiting to cut up the trees that the boys brought out to him from different parts of the woods. The brothers always worked separately. "You never work together," says Earle, "so you don't hit each other."

It could have been an hour, no one knows, that Scott lay there with his back and neck broken, all but three ribs in pieces, his sternum cracked, his lung pierced, and internal bleeding so bad he was drowning on dry land. Earle recalls perfectly how the professionals would later explain it: "When the tree hit him, it was like somebody took a shotgun and shot him, but inside. No blood coming out; it wasn't gory or anything. It just blew his bones and his ribs right apart."

After initially losing consciousness, Scott came to, and, for a brief window of time between the hit and the chaos and unspeakable pain that would kick in soon, there was silence.

There's a lot about that morning that's just a blur to Scott, but he distinctly remembers looking up into the thick ceiling of leaves. It was a wet, foggy spring morning, sometime around 8:00 on May 25, 1999. He also knows for sure that, "I didn't hear nothin'. It was just misting a little that day. I hear the skidder idling, and I'm thinking, *I gotta go to work.* I thought, *I have to get up for work.* But then the sound just keeps getting louder and louder, and I realized I was in trouble. I couldn't breathe. And y'know how people say they see the light? I actually did. It was like, I had to make a choice: come or go. I'm not lying to you. It was like a big, bright light. And it felt real comfortable. I had the sensation that I could go toward it or not. But I knew I really had to see my wife and kids again. I had unfinished business or something. The whole thing was, I wasn't alone there, even though I was. And I wasn't scared at all during the whole thing. I was never scared. I'm lying there and I can't breathe and I can't move and I wasn't scared."

You can think of it as a gift really, that Scott got to float in that brief space in time, because it was that space that would forevermore bookmark his life as the dividing line between "before" and "after." And the immediate "after" would be as rough as a life could get—one extreme after another of pain, terror, embarrassment, humiliation, frustration, anger, sadness... it goes on and on. But for that one pause, he was alone without feeling alone.

No matter how many people you talk to about Scott, you hear the same thing over and over: "I don't think I could handle it the way he has." It is a visceral, understandable reaction to the horror of what he experienced. It's just impossible for people to imagine how they would respond in a similar situation, and, except for his sister Renee, no one wants to find out, ever. (Renee has said time and again that she wishes the accident had happened to her instead of him.) They also say it out of respect for and amazement at how Scott has handled the aftermath. Knowing him and the life he led, not a single person would have blamed him if he hadn't managed quite so well.

"You've got to remember who you're dealing with," says his cousin, Bud DeMatties. "He's a logger, a guy who ran his own business and did everything himself."

"I've known Scott all my life," says brother-in-law, Keith Wood. "Being a lumberman is awful hard work, and it has to be hard knowing that you can't do your own work anymore. I think that would bother me the most, facing the fact that you can't just get out there and do all your own stuff."

"I enjoy what I do. I look forward to going to work every morning," says brother-in-law, Bill MacGlashan, also a logger from a family of loggers. "Scott was the same way. He and I talked it over, and, if the roles were reversed, he would have done the same as me—he would have gone right back to it."

Scott is and always will be a man of the woods. Growing up, he was and, in a lot of ways always will be, an Adirondack kid. The youngest of John and Gertrude's five children, he never cared much for school—hated it actually—but he loved sports, and he loved to work.

He was an especially gifted soccer player, earning MVP honors his senior year at North Warren High. And from the time he was thirteen, Scott, like Earle, learned from his dad to drive trucks, and began helping out in his dad and Uncle Jim's gravel business and, later, in the family logging business, Remington Brothers. Scott thought that running big equipment was just the greatest, and as he got older, he also found that he had an extremely good head for business. He bought Remington Brothers from his dad and uncle before he was thirty.

Scott didn't just live to work in the woods, he lived to play in the woods. He has craved hunting, camping, and snowmobiling since he was little, and can tell you one story after another of wild times and near-death experiences.

"Killed his first buck at fourteen and his first bear when he was sixteen!" beams his mom, Gert.

Scott remembers that bear plain as day. "I was on this rock. I had a Thirty-two Special, the kind you see on the Westerns. I saw it coming toward me. I shot and the thing stood up on its hind legs and growled. Then it ran right straight at me. And I hit it four times and saw blood coming out both sides. It dropped not more than a hundred paces from me. I was terrified! *Terrified*. I was shaking. Then my dad comes up and says, 'What are you *doin*'?' I said, 'There it is, Dad!'"

Then there was that time "when we were younger. I was driving a Jeep with my cousins down Hickory Hill Mountain. Rolled it, went over five times. Threw us all out."

And just a year before the accident, camping with his best friends after some serious partying: "My friends, we set up a hunting camp over in state land, took dead trees, threw a tarp over it, had a wood stove, and almost died in there one night. Yeah, the ground caught fire under the wood stove. It's the middle of the night, and my friend, Ted Meade, says, 'Hey, it's smoky in here.' And I said, 'Naa, go back to sleep, we're all right.' I didn't even open my eyes up, but I tell you, when he turned the flashlight on and said, 'No, come on!' you couldn't see from me to you. We ripped the sides of the tent off and immediately got out. My brother-in-law starts puking, 'cause once you hit the oxygen with all the smoke, y'know. *Real* terrible. 'Course, the alcohol probably didn't help either. If we didn't wake up, we probably woulda died of smoke inhalation. Teddy saved our lives that night."

Scott's not kidding when he says, "I got a lot of stories."

Now Scott's making a different kind of story. It's about how he clawed his way back from a nightmare—an accident pure and simple—that shattered his body in one unfair, unexpected moment. It's a story of the sheer guts and determination that he dragged out of God-knows-where, deep within himself, on just another day at work, when he came face-to-face, first with death itself, and then with a paralyzing outcome that felt like death to a guy who could never sit still.

"He's one of probably the toughest individuals I've ever run into," says David Osterberg, who was operations manager for Finch, Pruyn & Company, the mill that Scott was subcontracting for when he was hurt. "To have gone through that and still have the attitude he's got, *that's* resilience."

"I think anyone, even on the fringes of Scott's accident, had to realize they've witnessed a miracle," says cousin Bud. "You really don't have to be that close to the issues and know the in-depth details of what happened. If I tell a friend about what happened in the briefest conversation, I think they realize it's just a miracle that he even survived."

A lot of people look at Scott as something of a miracle. But this is not just the story of one man. It's also a story about the magic and transformative power of human connections. It's a reminder that life is a busy, two-way street, and that maybe the whole reason we're put on this earth is to reach out to others and *allow* them to reach in to us. That's why this is also about what a family did, what a town did, what a bunch of friends did to give strength to a guy who needed it, and to help drain the tragedy out of a tragic situation. And it's about what Scott has turned around and done in return for his friends, family, neighbors, and millions of other people who, for one damned unlucky reason or another, ended up in the same boat as he did.

Part I

By many measures, logging is the most dangerous occupation in the United States. The tools and equipment used in logging, such as chain saws and logging machines pose hazards wherever they are used. As loggers use their tools and equipment, they are dealing with massive weights and irresistible momentum of falling, rolling, and sliding trees and logs. The hazards are even more acute when dangerous environmental conditions are factored in, such as uneven, unstable or rough terrain, inclement weather including rain, snow, lightning, winds, and extreme cold, and/or remote and isolated work sites where health care facilities are not immediately accessible...

Occupational Safety & Health Administration
U.S. Department of Labor

1 .

Gearing Up Again

The casseroles began arriving around 3:30 in the afternoon. One by one, over the next thirty to forty minutes, cars and pickups crackled up the steep, gravel driveway to the flat area in front of Scott's lovely log home, which sits nestled into a hillside surrounded by trees.

Scott's a party guy, but this isn't a birthday, anniversary, neighborhood pig roast, or any other excuse to hang out with friends and family. It's business. This is Sunday, November 10, 2002, the second meeting of the organizing committee for Scott's annual spring fundraiser. This year's fundraiser, scheduled for March 29, 2003, will be his fourth, and, if it's like the last three, it will blow everyone's predictions about how many people will show up and how much money can be raised from a small, tight-knit community deep in the Adirondack Mountains of New York State. What started as a simple declaration by Scott, when he returned home in the summer of 1999 from the Kessler Institute for Rehabilitation, has become a veritable

5

institution in and around the tiny town of Brant Lake, New York.

Still wracked with pain and strapped into a hard, plastic body brace, he told his sister, Renee, that he was not about to spend the rest of his life in a wheelchair, and he didn't want all the friends he had just made at Kessler to spend their lives in wheelchairs either. Too many of them were a lot younger and a lot worse off than he was. That was the day Scott and Renee decided that they weren't going to sit around and wait for other people to do all the work to make a cure possible. They wanted to raise money and send every dime to The Christopher Reeve Paralysis Foundation. They had done some checking and liked that Christopher Reeve supported scientists and doctors who were doing the most daring research to get people back on their feet.

Scott's homecoming from Kessler, after nearly twenty days in the hospital and two months of grueling rehab, was a bittersweet time, a swirl of intense physical and emotional ups and downs. Still, he just picked up the phone one day and called Jimbo's. Sitting right on the shores of Brant Lake, Jimbo's is a cavernous 10,000-square-foot dining hall built out of honey-colored wood with a big stone fireplace. The manager at the time immediately agreed to donate the restaurant and provide food and beer for Scott's first event.

Stacey Dobbs, a friend of the Remingtons, who took over as the manager of Jimbo's in time for Scott's second fundraiser, has become one of the loyal troops who have helped to make the event a year-after-year success. Stacey remembers the first time she got Scott's call. "He just said, 'Listen, this is what I want to do and this is the date I'm looking for and what can you guys come up with?' So I went to my boss and said, 'This is a really good cause, a local, someone we need to support.'"

Stacey jumped into action. She called her family and her vendors. "I also come from a very close family," she says, "and they're all in the restaurant and hospitality business." Everyone said yes; everyone gave. For Stacey, it was hardly a tough sell. "Scott's an incredible guy. An *incredible* guy. His smile, when he used to walk into the room, he'd be smiling. Now he wheels into the room and he's smiling and he's always glad to see everybody. As many things as he's gone through, he's a heck of a lot of fun. He knows that he's gonna live life to the fullest."

Since the Scott Remington Family & Close Friends Spinal Cord Research Benefit kicked off in 2000, just about nine months to the day after Scott's accident, it has consistently drawn a crowd of more than 500 people, some from surrounding states. People even showed up in droves in 2002, when Scott was worried sick because they had scheduled the benefit on the same day as a major business expo in nearby Glens Falls. Each year, cars stretch so far up and down both sides of Route 8 in Brant Lake that the committee has had to run a shuttle to get all the people to Jimbo's. And every year, around 200 businesses have donated items to raffle.

Like just about everybody else, Scott's friend, Jill Wilson, is amazed that "all that stuff just keeps coming every year." And it's great stuff—vacations, camping equipment, canoes, fireplaces, four-wheelers, and tons of gift certificates.

Stacey can hardly believe it either—the collective, relentless generosity. Jimbo's owner, Jim Himoff, and his wife, Sue, donate the restaurant every year and nearly all the food. Rick Davidson at Davidson Brothers, a pub and microbrewery in Glens Falls, donates beer. Vendors contribute food, drinks, cups, mugs, plates, you name it. And there are businesses and local residents who simply write checks directly to Christopher Reeve's foundation.

"The benefit is usually supposed to be from one to six o'clock, but people are there till eleven o'clock at night," marvels Stacey. "I'm not kidding, there's probably six to eight different bands and they all play for free, too. Every year, people just hang out. Then there's the raffle, and I mean the raffle takes practically two hours. There's just tons of stuff, thousands and thousands and thousands of dollars worth of stuff that people donate. And all the money we make goes to the cause. It's all pure profit."

Everyone was pretty sure that the first benefit would be successful. After all, Scott, his friends, and his family had pulled it off soon after Scott's accident, when the trauma of his experience was still so raw. But year after year? Scott's first three fundraisers had sent a total of more than $71,000 to the Christopher Reeve Paralysis Foundation—an amount no one predicted, especially from a place like this.

Calling Brant Lake a "town" is generous. This is a hamlet of about 1,200 permanent residents. On one side of downtown is a small antique shop, post office, general store, firehouse, auto body shop, and town hall. On the other side of the street is a pond with a little beach. Drive through the town on a hot summer day, and the sound of kids playing in the water drowns out anything that passes for traffic noise, even though the area swells in the summer with vacationers. Brant Lake and the neighboring towns of Chestertown and Pottersville all share North Warren High School, where Scott's 1984 graduating class had forty students.

The success of Scott's event is the result of tremendous goodwill—very small towns in and around Brant Lake with very big hearts. It is also the result of an astounding amount of legwork and commitment—a very small committee with very big energy. "The committee" is roughly a dozen of Scott's family and friends. Meetings start in October and continue like clockwork every month until the event gets closer, then they're every two weeks, then every week up to the big day. Everyone has assigned jobs—printing, stuffing, licking, publicizing, soliciting—it's a well-oiled machine honchoed by Scott's sister, Renee, organizer *extraordinaire*.

Renee has saved every press clipping, letter, photograph, note, flyer, and receipt from every fundraiser, and preserved them all in separate plastic sleeves in a series of labeled binders. Before every meeting, she mails out reminders. At every meeting, she has an agenda.

This year, she's upped the efficiency quotient by dividing the team into subcommittees—raffle committee, flyer committee, T-shirt committee, letter writing committee, advertisement committee, entertainment committee, and decorating committee. Of course, with their small group, everyone is doing double and triple duty, and Scott is assigned to just about all of them. He may be the Chief Inspiration Officer of this business, but, make no mistake, he's no figurehead. This is business, and there's no slacking.

Of course, this wouldn't be a Remington event—even a business meeting—if it weren't also fun. Everyone gathers in Scott's great room, a high-ceilinged living room that flows into a kitchen area where potluck dishes line the counters wall-to-wall. With plenty of Labatt Blue on hand, it gets hard to hear over the pre-meeting chatter.

This night, before things get into full swing, Renee isn't laughing that her husband, John, crashed her computer, sending tons of benefit-related data into oblivion, but she can't help cracking up when John admits to the crowd that he did it trying to load free software of the game show, *Who Wants to Be a Millionaire?* Then they embarrass their daughter, Joss-Elyse, a pretty high-school freshman whose straight brown hair falls just below her shoulders, when they brag about her latest field hockey and basketball exploits and tell everyone how great she looked at the recent semi-formal. Joss promptly hops off the chair she's sharing with her dad and parks herself on the couch to watch NASCAR with the sound turned down low, so she can keep Uncle Scott up to date on *The Man*, Jeff Gordon.

And, like fishermen who just have to share stories about the "ones that got away," you can't have a room full of hunters without hearing the latest big-game tales. The best is the one that Scott tells everyone, half laughing and half shouting over competing conversations, about seeing a buck—"had to be about a five-pointer"—right outside his own house the other night. He grabbed his rifle, wheeled out onto the deck and was sure he could get it by aiming through the rails. "I had the scope right on it!" he laughs, "and then, BANG! I heard the wood fly. Took a chunk right outta the deck!" To every guy who comes into the room, he tells him: "Grab a Labatt's and go check out the hole in the deck!"

Says Scott's oldest sister, Denise, making the fundraiser happen takes a lot of work over about a seven-month stretch. "But it's fun. We always get together at Scott's house and everyone brings a dish to pass." During the year, committee members, alone and in groups, also take the show on the road, visiting scores and scores of businesses, thanking them in person for past support and asking for their support again. Scott's neighbor, Wendy Meade, loves to make the rounds with Scott and Renee, visiting businesses, picking up T-shirts and other supplies, and handing out flyers. Scott usually drives, parking on some main street in one of many little towns while Wendy and Renee walk in and out of stores. They have a blast, she says, and "we *always* make sure we go to lunch somewhere." Sometimes Wendy's husband Ted comes along. He's known Scott since they were kids and hunted with him since forever, and it's just fun when they're all together. "We spend a lot of days with Scott and Renee, sorting out items to be raffled and whatever's necessary to help out," says Wendy. "Four years ago, I would never have thought I'd be involved in such a volunteer project. It gives me a great feeling that I help out for such a great cause. I love it."

Ed Jay, married to Scott's cousin, Chris, feels exactly the same. The family calls him "Mr. PR" because of all the work he does. "I look forward to this event so much!"

he says. "I spend days and days going to hundreds of businesses from Lake George to South Glens Falls. I go to every business I can see, any rinky-dink place. I mean, Chinese restaurants, hair salons, a company that rents out restaurant supplies, pizza places, sporting goods, gas stations, it doesn't matter to me, and it doesn't matter whether they give a gift certificate or a cash donation. Last year, I went into a big plumbing place and they donated an $800 gas heater unit! I get a fabulous response, even after 9/11, after people had given so much to all the victims and firemen and the policemen. I never really get a door shut in my face. It's all for Christopher Reeve's foundation. It's going to spinal cord research. It's not like Scott takes *anything*."

After three home runs, you'd think that Scott would be as confident as Renee is organized. No way. Every year, his blood pressure spikes as the date gets closer. He worries about everything, but, above all, about whether anyone will show up. "Every year I just hope it'll all come together, but I get so nervous. Any little bit of money helps, that's the way I look at it." There's no relaxing until the cars pull up to Jimbo's, and he sees for himself the steady stream coming through the door. And this year, there would be a special goal as well as a surprise contact from the Christopher Reeve Paralysis Foundation that would make his pulse race even more. The committee wants this to be the year that they raise enough to push their all-time total to $100,000—a hundred grand in four years. Their track record is impressive, but the goal requires that they figure out how to raise their one-year take to about $30,000.

What's more, just about two months before the big day, Scott will learn that the foundation has generously agreed to send a representative to *his* fundraiser to show a video and speak to the crowd.

On this particular Sunday, the meeting is planned for 4:00, and Renee gets things rolling on the dot. Scott's mom, Gert, will miss just this one meeting, because she's down in South Carolina with girlfriends, but everyone else is here—his dad, his sisters, and their husbands, Aunt Cil and Uncle Jim, cousins Chris and Ed Jay, and friends Wendy and Ted, Chris Johnson, Lynn Lewis, and Lynn's sister, Laurie. There is also a slew of kids. Joss is the oldest at fourteen. Throughout the meeting, their chatter and laughter is constant in the background, including the squeals of joy that come from three-year-old Melissa Jay, who spends most of the time on a blanket with Scott's daughter, Jenna, sledding down the basement steps.

Besides the regular progress reports from each subcommittee, there are some hot-button issues tonight. One is to nail down the four biggest prizes to be raffled off to people who purchase the twenty-five-dollar tickets. This year's grand prize is a trip to one of four destinations— Jamaica, Cancun, Las Vegas, or Orlando. Aunt Cil has done the heavy lifting on that one, getting an amazing deal from a travel agent. Still, the trip prize, like all of the grand prizes from years past, will be the benefit's biggest single expense.

The raffle committee reports that, for the other big prizes, they've secured a bathroom vanity, a chainsaw, and a salmon fishing trip to Lake Ontario. Renee reminds

Ed and Scott that they have to get busy and complete the form for the company that will be printing the raffle tickets. Renee cautions them to work quickly and carefully, making sure they stay within the printer's limits of only nine lines and thirty-five characters per line.

"Everybody on the raffle committee, listen up!" she shouts so she can be heard above the side conversations crisscrossing the room, "You need to figure out how to list all this information on the ticket. I don't know how you're gonna do that. That's up to you guys. We don't need grand details, all that will go on the flyers, but we have to get this done so they can be printed in time." Ed wonders if Renee can find the form they filled out last year so he can use it as an example. Not a soul is surprised when, without a thought, she opens the binder that's in front of her at the dining room table and yanks last year's form right out of its plastic sleeve.

Next item is the redesign of the flyer that will publicize the 2003 benefit. "OK, the flyer committee," Renee announces. "Is that me?" Scott asks. The whole room erupts in unison, "No!" and he cracks up.

But seriously, Renee continues, the committee has decided to make room on this year's flyer so they can include the names of the musical acts and some key, repeat donors like Davidson Brothers. "We have to give these guys publicity," she insists. "They give of their time every year, free of charge. We need to give back to these people." Everyone agrees. Then someone yells from the far side of the living room, "So we're using the same logo on everything?"

"Oh man, here we go!" Scott moans sarcastically, and the crowd is off to the races. The issue of the logo, which appears on the benefit flyers and T-shirts, is the evening's climax. The logo, drawn by Scott's good friend, Trish Jarvis-Weber, depicts a figure holding a chainsaw over a person in a wheelchair. The idea is that the wheelchair is about to be demolished, and Scott loves it. But Aunt Cil and Wendy have heard grumbling from folks around town, who think it looks like someone is about to chop off the head of the person in the chair. Scott can't believe that anyone would fail to get it. Renee suggests that maybe Trish could redo it with someone getting up from the chair and walking.

"I'm sure Trish would be happy to meet with the T-shirt committee," she says.

"I might not be able to make that meeting," Scott laughs, and the whole room laughs, too. Not wanting to be a fly in the ointment, though, he agrees to consult with Trish about an alternative drawing.

Then it's on to: how many T-shirts to order; how much to sell them for; whether the committee wants special Henley shirts to distinguish themselves as "staff" on the day of the benefit; and what color the shirts should be. Renee supports a darker color, pointing out that Steph's husband Keith "has a tendency to spill stuff."

"What's a Henley?" someone calls out. And Ted Meade, who's been standing quietly in the doorway to Scott's bedroom, gets a hand when he steps out with both arms raised and does a turn, modeling the Henley-style shirt he just happens to be wearing.

Renee then mentions that David Carmel has offered again to make a speech at the event. David's family owns a vacation house on the lake, and everyone in the room knows him well. Scott's cousin, Chris Jay, babysat for David and his twin brother, Jason, when they were little. Ted Meade is the second-generation caretaker of the Carmels' property, having taken over from his father, Bruce, and Ted's wife, Wendy, cooks for the family. David was twenty-six when he was paralyzed in an accident, just weeks before Scott was hurt. He spoke at their first fundraiser, and everyone agrees that he will enrich the day. Renee notes that he was "phenomenal" that first year.

Wendy follows up with a reminder that Jason has also made a remarkable offer to speak to the committee and anyone in the community with a spinal cord injury, about the status of spinal cord research. When David got hurt, Jason had been in his second year of medical school. The tragedy led him to shift his focus to neuroscientific research, which he now does at the W. M. Keck Center for Collaborative Neuroscience at Rutgers University in New Jersey. Everyone is touched by his offer, and, for the first time, they plan a get-together for the night before the fundraiser—a lasagna dinner at the town hall for themselves and disabled residents in the area, highlighted by Jason's special presentation. The evening should be the perfect precursor to the fundraiser, a relaxed affair with time to visit and eat, but with a purpose. The committee always wants Scott's fundraisers to be fun, but they never want people to forget why they are there, as if that were possible.

In that spirit, Renee tells the group that Jason's presentation will be "for *our* insight. We all sit here and put in all this effort, and we really have no clue what all our money is doing. This will give us an idea."

Then she just can't help adding, "And, speaking of presentations, we know Scott will just do *his* little thank you. I coulda *killed* him at last year's benefit. He takes the mike and says, 'Thank you, thank you. Now, my sister will say a few words.' I coulda killed him!" Looking at Scott square in the face, she reminds him, "If I'd had a few minutes to think about it, you woulda been dead."

With a sheepish grin and a shrug, Scott's got no excuses. "Hey, you know I can talk to anyone, but I just can't talk in front of people. My heart gets goin'…"

The agenda wraps up with discussion about: entertainment for the children, since Tookie the Clown will be unavailable this year; new strategies for selling raffle tickets in the weeks leading up to the benefit; and, of course, the date of the next meeting.

Then it's on to dinner, and everyone makes the circuit through the kitchen, tasting some of this and some of that, and Scott makes sure that no one misses the fresh venison that he's been slow-cooking for hours in his Crock-Pot. He wheels around the room, making plans with Ed to get that ticket form done, telling the kids to please not take candy into the playroom, and negotiating with his sisters to figure out what night they'll each have their dad over for dinner while their mom's away.

He's the life of the party, which isn't surprising to anyone who knows him. It's only surprising that he's a life at all.

2.

"A widow maker, so they call 'em"

T he morning of May 25, 1999 was like any other
work day. Scott, his brother, Earle, and his dad,
John—whom everyone knows as Bull, "because he's always
been such a hard worker," says his wife, Gert—were up
before dawn. Earle and his dad woke around 5:30, met up
at the garage on the outskirts of town where Scott stored
his trucks and equipment, and drove together in one of
Scott's pickups to the job site up north. Scott didn't ride
with his dad and brother that day.

Scott was the baby in the family, but he was the boss
since he'd bought his dad and uncle's logging business,
Remington Brothers, back in 1993 at the age of twenty-
eight, renaming it Remington Logging. This day he was
up at 4:30 and drove straight to the garage. He hopped in
his pulp truck, a huge, tri-axle truck with a tandem pup
trailer that he used to haul timber to the various mills and
lumberyards. He drove to the Nice 'n Easy in Chestertown,

where he grabbed a cup of coffee, then fueled up the truck before heading up to the worksite.

Scott had hired a guy to drive the pulp truck, but the driver had quit a week or two before, and, when you're the boss, says Scott, "you do everything, double and triple duty if that's what it takes." Driving the truck was certainly much easier and safer than felling trees, but Scott didn't care much for the driving. "I'd rather be in the woods any day," he says.

Scott drove the truck up Blue Ridge Road, a winding two-lane artery with forestland on both sides, then turned off onto the gravel logging road and drove about another three miles to the job site. Scott didn't expect to be cutting that day. Instead, he planned to load the truck with around 90,000 pounds (roughly 12 cords) of timber that they'd cut the day before, and haul it to the Finch, Pruyn & Company mill down in Glens Falls. The work site was north of Brant Lake between the towns of Blue Ridge and North Hudson, part of the 166,000 acres of Adirondack Forest managed by Finch, Pruyn and thinned regularly by loggers like the Remingtons.

Company foresters are constantly inspecting the forests, putting paint marks on specific trees so the loggers know which ones the company wants to be cut. The lowest quality trees are harvested as pulp for paper, and higher quality trees are milled for lumber. In marking the timber, the foresters are also working to upgrade the overall quality of the forest by weeding out the "junk wood" and damaged timber, and making it easier for the forest to regenerate.

Scott, Earle, and Bull were working in an area that was part of a "beech salvage cut." Beech is a poor quality "weed species," so most of it ends up as pulp for paper or as wooden plugs in lawn furniture. The foresters were trying to clean out the stand to make way for more desirable growth.

Driving to work that day, Scott felt an extra rush. He had gotten word that a new circle-saw he'd ordered had arrived at the dealer, and he couldn't wait to pick it up later that day. Under Scott's management, Remington Logging was on a roll, and this was Scott's latest investment—a powerful saw that could cut felled trees into logs with the push of a button, freeing the men from the time-consuming, labor-intensive, and dangerous practice of cutting timber by hand with chainsaws. Years later, thinking back on that day, Scott shakes his head and his voice gets quiet as he talks about that saw. He still can't believe he never got to use it even once.

Scott beat his dad and Earle to the site. He fired up the loader that grabs logs in its giant claw and lifts them onto the pulp truck, but he soon realized that the load would be short. So, when Earle and Bull arrived, Earle headed into the woods to continue cutting, and Scott decided to go, too. That way, they could top off the delivery more quickly, and Scott could get on the road.

Their morning routine was always pretty much the same. Starting at about 7:00, the brothers would head out into different parts of the forest where they'd fell trees and trim off the branches with their chainsaws. Then they'd grab a bunch of the downed trees with their skidders and bring the loads out to Bull. A skidder is a four-wheel drive vehicle with a winch and heavy cable hanging off the end. The guys would drag the cable out to a downed tree, encircle the tree with a chain attached to the cable, and secure the chain with a hook. Then they'd drag the cable to the next tree, wrap it with a chain, and so on. When they retracted the cable back into the winch, it would gather the timber together in a tight bunch that they could drag out of the woods.

Bull waited at the header, a flat, open area beside the logging road, where he'd use a chainsaw to cut up the trees the way the mill wanted them—in various lengths ranging from four to twenty feet. Cutting was second nature to Bull, who used an experienced eye and a four-foot measuring stick to get the optimal number of cuts out of each tree.

The men always took a break around 9:00 for coffee and sandwiches. And it was just about nine when Earle came out with his third hitch of the morning, but Scott hadn't come out once. Bull really didn't need to tell Earle to go check on his brother. Earle still remembers, "I just get this gut feeling, and I leave the skidder and walk in."

It had been raining and it was foggy in there, and Earle wasn't sure where Scott was. The forest was dense, and except for birds, the breeze, and the intermittent drizzle, the Remingtons were making the only sounds for miles in all directions. So Earle moved quietly, trying to catch the hum of Scott's equipment. He hiked up a rise about a half-mile in, when he latched onto the sound of a motor and followed it till he saw the skidder. But where in the world…?

Earle walked around back of the machine, and there was Scott, "lying like you lay in bed, y'know, on your back, with his head and neck on the tree."

Earle thinks that Scott was in shock, yet he was conscious and eerily lucid. Scott still remembers with some amazement, "I waved to him. I just flipped my arm up, and I said, 'I broke my back. I can't feel my legs. You're gonna need to go get help. And if I don't make it," he added, "tell Cindy and John and Jenna that I love them."

Earle knew right away that his brother had it right, and he cringes at the memory of it. Scott's legs were pinned up behind him against his back in a sickening fashion. When he fell backward from the impact of the tree, he literally folded back in half. Earle could only guess at the extent of Scott's injuries, but there was no doubt that Scott's back had to be broken. And even though Scott was wearing a bright red, hooded sweatshirt, like he always did during hunting season, Earle saw a deep, unnerving indentation in Scott's side. "You could've put your hand in it. It was caved right in and I knew right then his ribs are gone."

Scott was coughing and "phasing in and out." Earle could hear a gurgling sound, the result of massive internal bleeding and a punctured lung. It was getting harder and harder for Scott to draw breath, but he kept struggling to talk, making Earle promise to get hold of Cindy and the kids, and telling Earle he felt numb. And then, as he teetered on the brink between here and gone, the next thing out of Scott's mouth just about blew Earle's mind. It was, "I'm sorry."

"He was choking on his own blood was what he was doin'," says Earle. Yet Scott suspected—no, he *knew*—that his brother had to be suffering, too, reliving a recurring nightmare. Earle couldn't believe that his brother would think of such a thing at a time like this, and urged him gently, "Don't be sorry."

About fifteen years before, when Earle was just twenty-three, he frequently logged with two brothers, John and Roger. They were all down in Fort Ann, about forty miles southeast of Brant Lake, cutting firewood on Valentine's Day. The wind was blowing hard and Earle was loading the skidder when John came running out of the woods yelling to Earle that a tree had fallen on his brother. Earle tore into the woods and, to this day, he has nights when he wakes up screaming from what he saw. Roger was pinned under a big piece of tree, like the one that hit Scott, "widow makers we call 'em," says Earle, "and it squished him like a piece of paper. Like nothin' you ever want to see. It was gory. He was a real good friend of mine. I worked with him a lot of years, him and his brother. The three of us. But it just pushed all the guts out of him, every hole he had in him, his ears, his mouth, his eyes. Nothin' you want to see."

It still moves Earle deeply that Scott understood. "With my brother, one of the first things he says is, *I'm sorry*, 'cause he knows I seen."

Scott also begged his brother to help him... to move him... to do *anything*. Earle didn't dare. That decision was fateful. The family wouldn't know until Scott had been through a battery of CAT scans that his neck—just like that treetop—had been hanging by a thread. The slightest comforting gesture could have killed him or paralyzed him from the chest down. Only a week before, Earle, Scott, and Bull had completed a first aid course required by their insurance company, and Earle had been instructed never to touch a guy who he even suspected of a spinal cord injury. "I knew right then I couldn't move him. I didn't dare to," he says. "So, what do you do?" Earle told Scott, "just lay there and pick a point and stare at it, and don't move a muscle till somebody gets here." Words to live by.

Earle also knew that Scott was running out of time, and he "started getting really nervous." He was trying to keep Scott awake, "cause he'd phase in and out and I knew enough not to let him go under." Earle couldn't call for help because Scott's cell phone was in the pulp truck, and it was doubtful that he could get a signal up there anyway. He didn't want to leave his brother alone, but he had no choice. Scott said OK. Earle ran out to the header to tell his dad that Scott was in big trouble.

Not a minute before, a truck had pulled up with two Finch, Pruyn foresters making their regular rounds to check in with the various logging crews working that day. It was veteran district forester, Ray Saladin, showing the ropes to twenty-four-year-old Johnny Pratte, a district forester making his very first stop on his very first day in the field.

Ray was about to introduce Johnny to the Remingtons, when Earle came running out of the woods. For Earle, seeing those foresters was…. well, only the most amazing thing. He has no words to describe the feeling except, "Thank God, it was just a miracle."

No one's cell phone could catch a signal, so, leaving Johnny on the site to help, Ray raced down the logging road to the main road and drove another three miles until he reached the Adirondack Buffalo Farm—the first place he could find to call for help and alert the home office of the emergency. The Buffalo Farm was well known in the area, so he gave the paramedics directions from there to the entrance of the logging road, where Ray parked his pickup and waited to flag them down.

Meanwhile, Earle and Johnny had run back into the woods to be with Scott. Earle took off his chaps—the heavy leg coverings that the men are required by their insurer to wear to protect their legs from cuts—and he laid them on Scott to help him stay warm.

To Earle, it seemed like hours before help arrived. Johnny remembers that Scott was clearly in shock, but kept talking to them, saying the same things over and over—was he gonna be all right, he couldn't feel his legs, was he gonna be all right, he couldn't feel his legs, was he gonna be all right, he couldn't feel his legs ...

Earle and Johnny did their best in a situation that left them the worst kind of helpless. They stood inches from Scott, but they might as well have been miles away. "We knew we shouldn't move him," says Johnny. "There wasn't much I could do, but try to keep him calm." All they had was talk. So they tried to keep Scott awake and keep panic at bay.

"People don't really understand," Earle says, thinking back on those horrible moments, "unless you're right there on the spot. It's not like you're going down the road and find a wreck. Y'know, when you're on the road, there's people around. There's activity going on. When you're up in the middle of nowhere, and it's just woods, and there's nothing there that you can work with or anything, just rocks and trees, it's a totally different thing."

Earle went out to the road at one point to report to his dad, who was worried sick but staying put, because he was equally worried that paramedics wouldn't be able to find their way. Johnny ran back several times, too, once to get an extra shirt to help keep Scott warm, and, finally, *finally* to lead paramedics into the woods.

The first to arrive was emergency medical technician Sally Vinskus, who actually lived on Blue Ridge Road in North Hudson. When she first got the page, she called in for instructions, but the dispatcher mistakenly told her that the case was a broken back at the Buffalo Farm. Sally figured someone had fallen off the roof. When she got there, though, some men said, "Oh no, it's a fella up in the woods," and one of them led her up the road where Ray was stationed to direct her in. At sixty-seven, Sally was a squad veteran, but getting to Scott was a new kind of test. "It was a good half mile into the woods and on the side of a mountain," she remembers. "The first hundred feet or so was sheer mud. I mean *mud*. I was up to my knees, and it was black because of the skidders."

Johnny Pratte had taken her medical bag and led her about two-thirds of the way in, when the second paramedic, twenty-five-year-old, six-foot-four-inch John Strothanke, came galloping up beside them. "He had tremendous long legs and he just went up the side of that mountain like it was nothing," Sally recalls.

John reached Scott a minute or two before Sally, but it was apparently long enough for him to carefully unfold Scott's legs, because, when Sally reached the site, "to the best of my knowledge," she says, "his legs were straight." The two EMTs immediately fell into a rhythm, working in unison to do what they could until more help arrived. Sally's primary job was to stabilize Scott's head. She lifted it ever so slightly and straight up—*perfectly* straight up—to relieve the pressure on his neck, and cradled it in her hands while John worked from the chest down. John covered Scott to try to keep him warm, then took vital signs and tested his extremities. John asked Scott to squeeze his hands, then, moving down his body, he pressed on Scott's torso and legs to test for feeling, and asked him to try to move his toes and feet. John and Sally worked for about forty-five minutes before the rest of the crew arrived.

Finally, clinical care technician, Mary Sprano, arrived in an ambulance, which parked on the header while she hiked into the woods with additional equipment. Mary also remembers laboring to reach Scott. "It was terrible. It was very muddy, it was steep, and of course you're walking over trees and logs and brush and trying to step over rivulets of water running down. It was rough terrain."

Around that time, state troopers arrived, along with firemen from North Hudson and Schroon Lake, and David Osterberg, operations manager for Finch, Pruyn. Back at the company, Dave had heard a secretary trying to get hold of someone because there had been an accident. He got the location and raced over. "I walked up into the woods with the state troopers. Scott was lying there, and I said, 'Hey Scott, how you doin'?' He looked up and says, 'Hey Dave.' That was pretty tough."

Scott was remarkably coherent and calm, Sally remembers, telling them that he couldn't feel anything from the waist down. Sally and John decided that they had to get the log out from under Scott to get a cervical collar around his neck, but the log was too big to move. So, Dave held a coat to shield Scott's face, while someone else grabbed Scott's chainsaw and cut the tree, making a shorter piece that they slid out from under his head. "We were finally able to get the collar on him," says Sally, "and we tried to get him covered as much as we could because it was still rainy and the ground was cold and wet."

Scott was struggling to breathe and the paramedics knew they had to get him out of there. There were now roughly ten people around him, and they lined up four or five on a side and carefully lifted his body straight up just an inch or two off the ground, so paramedics could get a "vacuum mat" underneath him. Better in this case than a traditional backboard, the mat is six feet long with handles on either side and tiny Styrofoam pellets inside. Once it was underneath Scott, the paramedics used a pump that sucked the air out of it, so that it firmed up all around him—"like a vacuum pack of coffee," Mary explains— immobilizing him without putting too much pressure on his body.

It took everyone to get Scott down the mountain and out of the woods to the waiting ambulance. According to Sally, one group started carrying Scott down, and, when they got to roughly the halfway point, another crew took over. "He was a good size fellow and with the weight of it and the terrain it was a good idea to switch." On the way, Dave, who had just been elected to his local school board, tried to lighten the mood a bit, asking Scott, "So, did you vote for me?" He was dumbfounded that Scott actually responded and was still talking when they lifted him into the ambulance.

Mary and Sally rode with Scott and continued to take his vitals as they made the maddeningly slow ride down the logging road. Sally thinks it was at least a couple of miles out to the main road, and both she and ambulance driver, Tom Ringrose, clearly remember the frustration of that drive. "It was demanding, we had to go so slow," says Tom. There was Scott, fighting for time, and on the one hand, "we couldn't go fast enough," says Sally, "but the road was very rutted, and we didn't want him jostled any more." Finally they reached the main road, where they could pick up some speed to the Albany Med FLIGHT helicopter waiting a few miles beyond the Buffalo Farm in the big parking lot at Frontier Town, an abandoned Old West reenactment town.

All the while, Sally remembers how grateful she was that Scott "had a lot of spirit." "You have a lot of people who would be, 'Why did this happen to me? I have a bunch of kids. What's going to happen to me?' And he didn't. He just focused on being as calm as he could be, which was great, because when somebody's crying and carrying on, it makes our job that much harder."

Scott remembers being lifted out of the ambulance and the sh-sh-sh-sh sound of the helicopter blades. He's pretty sure it was just before they put him in the helicopter when someone said, "This is gonna hurt a little."

"They took a scalpel and sliced in between my ribs. Put the tube in to drain the blood out of my chest cavity. I do remember that, and then I was out. I woke up in the hospital in Burlington."

Earle and Bull took off even before the ambulance pulled out. They had to get out of there, find Gert, and get to the hospital. For some reason, maybe a stew of panic and worry, Bull thought he remembered the medics talking about speeding Scott to Glens Falls Hospital to be checked over and then maybe transferring him to Albany Med. But Earle distinctly remembers that, when the paramedics brought Scott out of the woods, they knew that Scott's time was slipping away. He needed the closest trauma center, and that was in Burlington, Vermont at Fletcher Allen Hospital. That's why Scott ended up flying north, while Bull and Gert would soon be flying *south* down highway 87 toward Glens Falls with Gert behind the wheel, praying that a trooper wouldn't catch her.

3.
The troop mobilization

Scott's accident set off a massive chain reaction. The news, as much as people could piece together anyway, flew from phone to phone to phone.

In the meantime, Bull and Earle had a mission—find Gert. They tried her at home. She wasn't there. Bull knew that she had been scheduled to work that day; Gert provided companionship and some home care to a woman in her nineties named Isabel. They drove to Isabel's, but Gert had already left. Luckily, there aren't many places to hide in Brant Lake, and they finally tracked her down at Brant Lake Supply, a garden center in town.

Gert had picked up four-year-old Dakota, her daughter Stephanie's little girl, and off they went to buy flowers. Gert and Dakota were wandering the rows of plants, when Gert heard someone calling, "Mom, Mom!" It couldn't possibly be anyone in her family, so she ignored it. Finally, she picked up a crate of flowers, looked up, and there was Earle standing in the distance. Gert hurried over to see what the...

Earle just didn't know how to tell her, so, "You gotta go with Dad," was all he could manage. Gert could only think, *it's Bull's mother.* Her mother-in-law had had several strokes, and that was the only reason she could imagine that she'd have to hurry off with Bull. She asked Earle, "What's the matter?"

He just said, "Go with Dad! Dad'll tell you."

Gert would have none of that. "You've *got* to tell me," she demanded. "No matter how bad it is, I've got to know where I'm going and why I'm going!"

So Earle told her, "It's Scott. They're airlifting him."

Gert can still feel the electric charge of the news. "To be honest with you, I don't know what I ever did with that crate of flowers. I don't know if I laid them down or if I dropped them."

Earle drove his parents to their house, and they took off immediately in their station wagon, but, again, in Bull's confusion, they headed due south for Glens Falls. Earle stayed at his parents' house with Dakota, waiting for his sister, Stephanie.

Bull is a grizzly of a man with a broad, white beard and the leather hands of someone who's at home in the woods and has spent his life working heavy equipment. Gert's a petite woman who stands about shoulder-height beside her husband, but when the two of them are on the move, she says, "I always drive." And that day, she surely did, pushing the needle past eighty. She tried desperately to keep her wits, leaning into the steering wheel and gripping the thing with white-knuckled determination as her brain flooded with maternal angst. "I was more worried about him being frightened, being alone. I knew Scott's wife, Cindy, was working—she was driving the mail on a rural route, and it's hard to find somebody unless you know the route. So my thoughts were—Scott is all alone. He's *got* to be frightened. If I could just be there and comfort him. That's all I ask. I didn't ask for miracles or anything."

Bull and Gert pulled into the hospital, hurried through the emergency entrance, and asked for Scott Remington. But the receptionist said, "There's no Scott Remington here." Gert was not about to wait around to get things sorted out; she asked to use the phone. "I figured, by now, Renee must know what's going on," says Gert. Renee is her second youngest and the family switchboard where Scott's concerned. No sister was ever closer to a brother than Renee is to Scott.

Just then, the hospital phone rang—a miracle that neither Gert nor Renee can believe. The hospital staffer answered, and it was Renee, saying, "My parents are going to be walking through that door and I need to talk to my mother!" The woman said, "Is her name Gert Remington? She's standing right here."

Renee had gotten a call from Cindy. Somehow, the folks at Finch, Pruyn had tracked Cindy down and let her know that Scott was being flown to Burlington. In fact, Steve Satterfield, the company's wood procurement manager, who knew Scott well and had worked with various Remingtons since 1979, instructed his assistant to tell Cindy to "sit tight." He was on his way to pick her up and take her to the hospital.

Renee told her parents, "You're at the wrong hospital, get back to my house fast!" Gert was on the case. "Believe it or not, it takes about thirty minutes to get from Glens

Falls to here," says Renee. "It seemed like they showed up in minutes."

When Renee, who is a registered nurse, had gotten the call from Cindy, it was about 1:00 in the afternoon, and she was putting on her uniform to go to work. Renee's husband, John Smith, had come home for lunch that day, and the two of them had just gotten back from a walk. Renee was frantic. She called her oldest sister, Denise, at work. Denise is the head housekeeper at Point o' Pines, a girls' camp in the summer and the site of Jimbo's Restaurant, which serves the camp in the summer and is open to the public the rest of the year.

Denise remembers that Renee was hysterical, and "they usually call *me* the hysterical one." Renee is the first to admit she was "in a panic, a total panic," when she told Denise that John was on his way to pick her up.

John kept repeating, "Relax, Renee, relax." Then, as if by reflex, Renee picked up the phone and called her minister. She told him, "I really don't know what's happening. Just pray. Get everyone to pray. I can't talk, I gotta go." She just felt so desperate, she didn't know what else to do.

Then she called her mom's house. Steph, who had just arrived to get Dakota, picked up the phone and relayed everything that Earle knew at the time. Through Steph, Earle told Renee that Scott couldn't move his legs and that he was choking on his own blood. Renee, the nurse and sister, felt her heart break.

When they got off the phone, Earle left to get his girlfriend, Pooch, who was working at a local flower shop, and the two of them headed to Burlington.

Denise was waiting at Point o' Pines for Renee's husband, John, to arrive and desperate to get word to her own husband, Bill, who is also a logger and was working at a site out on Stock Farm Road near Chestertown. Thankfully, Bernie Bolton, a close family friend and head of maintenance at the camp, was working that day. Bernie also runs an excavating business with one of Scott's best friends in the world, Chris Johnson. Chris practically grew up at the Remingtons' house. He's Scott's brother in every way but blood, and—as far as Gert's concerned—he's one of her own. "Number six" she calls him. Bernie and Chris had been grading the golf area at the camp when they got the news from Denise. They told her not to worry, they'd find Bill.

Bill was on the header at his job site. He was running his saw, wearing protective earmuffs, and didn't hear them drive up. Chris was so agitated when he jumped out of the truck that, without thinking, he ran up and put his hand on Bill's back, and that definitely got Bill's attention. Bill always works alone, so the touch nearly gave him a heart attack. And with the live chainsaw in his hand, thank goodness he was able to hit his chain brake.

He turned and saw Chris, and remembers, "It took me several seconds to calm him down so I could understand what he was telling me. I got that somebody was hurt. I thought my wife, Denise, had been in an accident or something. I finally grabbed him and sat him down, and said, 'You gotta compose yourself and tell me what you're trying to tell me, 'cause I don't understand you!'"

On hearing the news, Bill immediately gathered his stuff and headed to Renee's. Chris and Bernie took off to get Chris's girlfriend, Lynn Lewis, who had dated Scott in high school and had remained his friend ever since. Bernie in his truck, and Chris and Lynn in their car, drove to Renee's, too, to be with the family.

Renee's driveway was filling up. It was a frenzy of family members, neighbors, and friends. Gert can't remember how many people converged there. "There were so many people offering to take us and just throwing money in the car, because they said they didn't know how long we'd be gone and what we'd be needing." That image sticks with all the Remingtons—friends emptying their pockets and throwing money through the car windows.

At the time, nobody was sure where Stephanie was, but she was on her own mission. When she had picked up Dakota and learned of the accident from Earle, at first she thought the best thing to do would be to stay around town and look after Scott and Cindy's children, John and Jenna. Earle nixed that idea right away, telling her, "Scott's hurt real bad, and we don't think he's gonna make it." After talking to Renee, it was decided that Denise's husband, Bill, would go to Steph's house and wait there for Steph and her husband, Keith, and the three would drive together to Burlington. Steph then left to find Keith at the main cemetery in town. Keith is the caretaker for all seven cemeteries in the area, and was mowing the grass at the time. Steph was crying as she hurried up to him, and Keith was sure something had happened to one of the kids. Steph told him Scott was hurt real bad and might even be dead.

When something like that happens, says Keith, "you can't go fast enough." He took off for the highway department, informed his boss, and punched out. Steph and Keith got home, where they met up with Bill, arranged for relatives to take Dakota and pick up their son, Adrian, at school, and took off for the hospital.

Meanwhile, the news was racing through Brant Lake and the surrounding area. In the community that day, friends were calling friends, were calling aunts, uncles, and cousins, sharing what bits and pieces they knew. Even strangers in shops, homes, worksites, and anywhere else that people gather, were asking, "Did you hear?" That is, if you can call them strangers in an area where the Remington name had been a fixture for generations. Neighbors and friends instantly made commitments to stay in touch, look after the Remingtons' houses, and care for their children.

"News just really travels fast," says Stacey Dobbs, long-time friend of the family and manager of Jimbo's. "The news I got was that they didn't think he was going to make it. Knowing the Remington family—I mean they're an extremely tight group—everybody's heart just went out to them. It was extremely sad. Everybody was just really scared that he wasn't going to make it."

Two of those who kept the home fires burning while the Remingtons were in Burlington were Ted and Wendy Meade. They had been neighbors of Scott and Cindy for more than ten years, and Ted had known Scott all his life. Just a year behind Earle in school, Ted and Earle used to pal around as kids. As neighbors, the two couples spent a lot of time together, and Ted and Scott became regular hunting buddies. To Scott's kids, the Meades' house was as familiar as their own.

It was about 3:00 in the afternoon when Wendy got a call from Earle's ex-wife, Micky, who said that Scott might be hurt. Micky heard when she walked into the health center in Chestertown for an appointment, and people were talking. Micky was calling to see if Wendy knew anything.

Wendy was stunned. "There's just no way this is happening," she thought. "How could it happen twice in five weeks?" Her husband Ted is the caretaker at Brant Lake Farm, the vacation home of the Carmel family from New York City. The Carmel's twenty-six-year-old son, David, had been vacationing in Mexico when he was paralyzed in a diving accident on April 17, and she and Ted were devastated by the family's tragedy. Wendy called Scott's cousin, Chris Jay, to see if the news were true. Chris said yes, something happened, but she wasn't sure of the details.

"Within two minutes," says Wendy, "Chris called back and said that Scott was probably paralyzed." Wendy immediately called Ted at the farm. Working that day with his father Bruce and Randy Dooris—both of whom were friends and hunting companions of Scott's—Ted remembers that "we were all in the horse barn when we got the call."

When Ted got home, he and Wendy were dazed. The sadness, shock, and worry gave them both a sickening feeling. Wendy clearly recalls how surreal the world suddenly felt. "It's like our chests felt funny. We had this nervous, jerky feeling. The not knowing was awful." They never cooked dinner that night; eating was out of the question, and when they finally got their kids down and crawled into bed, they lay there in silence with their minds racing, yet not knowing what to think. Finally, Ted turned away, perhaps thinking that Wendy wouldn't realize why, but she knew he was crying silently for his friend.

In those first few days after the accident, Chris and Ed Jay, Scott's cousin and her husband, opened their home as a refuge for Scott and Cindy's children. John was just eight and Jenna six. Stephanie and Keith's children, Dakota and Adrian, stayed with them for a few days, too. The Jays also became "the focal point for the rest of the family," says Ed. "People called constantly to find out what was going on. Our phone rang off the wall."

Both Chris and Ed "kept the children busy and just kept things very stable for them." And when John and Jenna finally learned what happened, Chris and Ed helped them deal. John essentially withdrew. The way Ed saw it, the little boy just "went into a cocoon. He didn't want to hear what happened." Jenna, on the other hand, was hungry for information. She'd ask Chris, "What do you think they're doing right now? Is he gonna be alive when I see him?"

Scott and Cindy's good friends, Jill and Gary Wilson, found exactly the same thing when they took the children after several days. Family members, including Chris and Ed, were anxious to get up to Burlington, and, when Jill finally got in touch with Cindy to ask what she could do to help, they both decided that it would be best for the children to go there. "That wasn't a lot for us," says Jill, who was happy to help in any way.

Gary agrees. "We just opened the house to them. We wanted to give them roots. We felt that was important." John and Jenna lived with the Wilsons for about three weeks, and, "By the time they left," Gary says, "they were very comfortable. They'd come home from school and open the cupboard and get a snack. We made them feel at home." The children didn't discuss the accident much, but when they wanted to, Gary and Jill "didn't try to hide it or sugarcoat it."

Just as Chris and Ed had found, John was quiet. Whether he was in denial or just trying to be strong, he didn't want to talk or hear about it, whereas Jill remembers that Jenna "would have her bouts where she wanted to discuss it, and she talked about it in very blunt terms. She'd be very matter-of-fact about what happened."

On that first day, though, as the news sank in and the town prepared to keep vigil, six cars were speeding north. In each one, the air was thick with anxiety, everyone fearing the worst and hoping for… anything but the worst.

Some cars were quiet, their occupants lost in thought, concentrating to hurry the two-hour drive. In other cars, there was hushed talk, as everyone tried vainly to relieve the tension by endlessly replaying the same sketchy facts.

Steve Satterfield from Finch, Pruyn didn't know Scott's wife, Cindy, at the time, but he remembers that they talked constantly in the car. "She had no idea what condition he was in. Pretty much I tried to keep her spirits up. We talked quite a bit to pass the time." Cindy talked to Steve about Scott's family, her family, and about how she wished he'd gotten out of the business, as Steve "just tried to keep the time going by."

Renee will never forget that trip between Brant Lake and Burlington and the utter frustration of battling time and space. "I remember being on the road. And it's such a long road. It's all single lanes. Winding, country roads. There's no main highways from here to Burlington. And it seemed like forever."

Gert was squeezed into the back seat with Renee and Denise, reliving the simple but searing fears from her earlier, aborted trip down the highway. "I prayed out loud all the way that he would just be OK, that I could just get to him. I was just so afraid that he was going to die, because Bull had told me how bad he was hurt. I never asked that he wouldn't be paralyzed or anything, if I could just get there. It's almost like I wanted to be there to say good-bye. I just had to see him. I couldn't let him be alone. I didn't know where Cindy was at the time. I just didn't want Scott to be alone and be frightened. It's an awful feeling. I don't know if it's because I'm a mother. You just want to be there for them. If you could just touch them and say everything's going to be OK."

The modesty of her prayers could not have been more appropriate. Given what they would find in Burlington, she was wise to hope, but not for too much.

4.
The "after" begins

Scott's wife, Cindy, and Steve Satterfield were the first to arrive at the hospital. Steve stayed with Cindy so she wouldn't be alone. At one point, two nurses came out to the waiting area. One spoke to Cindy, while the other talked to Steve separately. "I've never seen anybody this bad," the nurse told him. "With this type of injury, I don't know if he's going to make it."

While Steve was talking to the nurse, Cindy wandered outside and was standing on the sidewalk crying, when the car with Scott's mom and dad, sisters Denise and Renee, and Renee's husband John pulled up. Seeing Cindy in tears, the first thing that hit Denise was that they were too late, "He's no longer with us." They gathered around Cindy, and she told them as much as she knew—Scott was alive, but being evaluated, and it didn't look good. Steve Satterfield came out to say hello to the family. They thanked him profusely for his help. Steve then turned to leave, assuring Cindy, "you're in good hands now."

The family moved inside, huddling in the waiting room. Within minutes it seemed, Renee heard, "Is Renee there? Is Renee Smith there?" A doctor was explaining Scott's status to Cindy, so that she could sign papers authorizing surgery, and she wanted Renee there to help her understand what was happening. The report was grim.

Before they had done a single CAT scan or X-ray, from just an external, visual check of Scott's body, the doctors saw what they called an "obvious step off at the T9-10 level." They could see the lump where the vertebrae at the mid-back or thoracic level were pushed apart.

The thirty-three vertebrae that run down the length of the back from the base of the skull to the tailbone form a bony, protective column that houses the spinal cord. The spinal cord, which is really an extension of the brain, is like a twisted rope of wires running down through the vertebral column with nerves, like pieces of wire, exiting through the sides of the vertebrae, sending signals and sensation to different parts of the body. Scott had a mid-thoracic crush injury. The bony vertebral bodies at that mid-point in his back did not just break, they also slipped clear out of alignment, cutting the cord at that spot. Whatever other injuries the medical staff would find from further tests, there was no doubt that that lower thoracic injury was what they call "complete," producing instantaneous cessation of feeling and control below that point.

Scott can remember, "When I woke up, I was on so many drugs and things were blurry. It was hard. I knew I was in bad shape, but I didn't think I wouldn't walk again. You keep telling yourself you'll be all right, you're strong, just keep fighting. And so much pain, so much pain. I couldn't move. It just hurt."

An especially cruel consequence of spinal cord injury is that the loss of function that the patient suffers on impact is only the beginning. The trauma sets off a chain of chemical reactions in the body that damage or destroy healthy cells that actually survived the initial injury. That secondary damage can continue for days or even weeks, exacerbating the loss of function.

One of those reactions is called *apoptosis*, which is, literally, preprogrammed cell suicide. Cell birth and death are natural processes, but some traumas, like spinal cord injury, mysteriously trigger apoptosis, setting off a cascade of events that lead healthy cells to start self-destructing.

At the same time, intense inflammation occurs at the site of injury, because the trauma also triggers the release of highly unstable molecules, known as free radicals. These molecules, which are natural byproducts of some functions like digestion, respiration, and stress, are missing an electron, and so they attack healthy cells to steal electrons from their molecules. Under "normal" circumstances, our bodies control this natural, predatory process of molecular damage, known as *oxidative stress*, because nutrients in our bodies called *antioxidants* attack and neutralize free radicals. But following a spinal cord injury, free radical production can be so intense that it overpowers our supply of antioxidants and leads to cell damage that expands outward from the lesion.

There are no surefire ways to halt what has been described as these "biological ripple effects," and a great deal of research is being done to address the damaging effects of the inflammation and apoptosis that occur in the wake of spinal cord injury. However, some clinical trials have suggested that the steroid *methylprednisolone* may be effective in limiting the secondary damage caused by inflammation, so many spinal cord injured patients are given large doses of steroids in the hours immediately after their accidents. Scott was one. Soon after he arrived at the hospital, his records show that he was "given a Dexamethasone (a brand of adrenal corticosteroid) bolus (a concentrated mass of ready-to-swallow medication) and started on a 24 hour steroid course."

In close succession, the cars began arriving—Earle and his girlfriend, Pooch; Steph, Keith, and Bill; Cindy's mother, sisters, and stepfather; and dear friends Chris Johnson and Lynn Lewis.

Denise went outside when she saw Steph's car drive up. Steph saw Denise crying and was sure that Scott was dead. Denise said no, but he was bad, and they were being allowed to see him right away.

The family remembers the nurses being so generous, letting them all go in to see Scott. Although the staff was trying to get Scott stabilized and evaluate him for surgery, "they were wonderful to us," says Gert. "They let us go into the room as many times as we wanted."

They all struggle for the words to describe what they saw. Scott's face and body were so bloated from the buildup of fluid and massive, trauma-induced swelling, he didn't look anything like himself.

Along with the disfiguring swelling, Renee can still see the "leaves all over his bed, and he was filthy dirty from the woods. There was blood saturating the sheets where they put the chest tube in when they were medevacing him. You had to really get down in his face to hear him, because he had a mask on and he was really so weak. I remember him asking me, 'What's my blood pressure?' And I said to him, 'It's better than mine.'"

Denise's husband, Bill, was struck by how gray Scott looked. "That was the one thing that concerned me," he says. As a former firefighter who had seen his share of tragedy and had worked the Jaws of Life in a number of severe automobile accidents, Bill "didn't like seeing that look."

Scott was conscious, but barely, straddling panic and remarkable rationality. Earle remembers the doctors leveling with Scott about his condition. They also instructed the family not to lie to Scott if he asked questions. "When they told him he was paralyzed," says Earle, "that was, oh man, so emotional."

Renee's husband, John, went in to see Scott, and "just to see him was devastating." John returned to the waiting room in a daze, and just then, he says, "They asked for Renee to come in. She might have had to sign some papers, and then she came back out and said that they think Scott's paralyzed. I just remember a lot of us saying that he won't want to live like that."

Gert is haunted by the memory of her boy's face. "He looked so frightened and in so much pain, and I just said, 'Close your eyes and try to get some rest.' I figured that if he closes his eyes, he might not notice the pain quite so bad. It was that frightening look on his face. I just wanted to pick him up like a little baby and cuddle him. I did touch him, and told him I loved him. He kept saying to me over and over and over again, 'Mom, if anything happens to me promise me that you'll watch out for Cindy and the children.' I said, 'Of course, Scott! I'll watch over them.'"

Scott urged Steph, too: "Help Mom with the kids." Steph is convinced that, at that moment, "he knew in his heart that he wasn't going to make it. But I said, 'You're gonna make it!'"

Scott's pal, Chris, was the last to arrive. He walked in to a somber scene of tears and helplessness. He talked to the family for a few minutes, then they told him he could go in and see his friend. "I was hesitant at first," he remembers. "You're walking in, and you don't know what you're gonna find. I really can't describe it. It's something that I wouldn't want to have to go through again. I just held onto his hand and told him everything was gonna be all right."

Some time later, the doctors came back with a new sense of urgency. A CAT scan revealed that Scott's neck was broken. His hospital records note a "comminuted fracture" (a fracture that breaks or splinters the bone into small pieces) at C6 and 7. Seven "C" or cervical vertebrae sit above the twelve thoracic vertebrae to form the portion of the spinal column in the neck and shoulders. Although Scott's thoracic injury further down was worse—it was no doubt the ground zero of impact, and doctors recorded it as an "overtly comminuted fracture dislocation at T9-10"—his cervical injury was more life-threatening.

Scott's cervical vertebrae were blown out, probably when he ricocheted backward and his neck landed on the tree, yet there was enough connective tissue and muscle remaining to hold the spinal cord in place... barely. The wrong movement of his head, even a reflexive twitch of his body, could have killed him or left him almost fully plegic, unable to move below the chest.

Still more tests showed a "burst fracture with slight (spinal) canal compromise" at the T7 level. In addition, his sternum, the bone running down the middle of his chest that should have been anchoring his ribs, was fractured, along with all but three of those ribs. As a result, blood had flooded into the space behind his sternum—between his chest wall and his heart. And one lung was perforated and filled with the blood that was leaking in from his chest cavity. The perforation was likely caused by a bone fragment that had exploded off his spinal column.

At one point, unable to locate Cindy, the hospital staff came to Renee with additional authorization forms. "But I'm not his wife," she told them.

"It doesn't matter," they said, "we need to take him." Time was slipping away.

Around 5:00 that evening, the surgical team was ready. Renee was the last one to talk to Scott. "He said to me, 'Promise me that you'll take care of Cindy, and tell the kids I love them.' And I remember I turned to him and said, 'I promise you I'll do that, but you have to promise me something, too—you have to fight! You fight to live and I'll carry through, and I won't leave you. I will not. I'll be here the whole way.' At that point, I felt like he needed more than what they could do for him. He needed to know that you gotta fight, in your subconscious, to live."

The family wouldn't see Scott again for nearly twelve hours.

In the operating room, the neck fracture was job one for his five-man surgical team. The first incision would be in the front of his neck, so Scott was lying face-up on the table. A tube was snaked down through one of his nostrils and into his trachea or windpipe to help him breathe. Doctors couldn't intubate through the mouth because that would require them to lift Scott's head back and hyperextend his neck to open his airway. Going in through his nose allowed them to send the tube straight down in a more direct route to Scott's windpipe while keeping his head and fragile neck in a neutral position.

Gardner-Wells tongs, which look like U-shaped ice tongs, were fixed by pins to either side of Scott's skull, and weights attached to the end of the tongs were hung over the table to provide spinal traction. Because the bony column that supported Scott's neck was broken, the muscles along the sides of his cervical spine were pulling on the rest of his vertebrae and threatening to yank the spinal cord out of its now precarious alignment. The doctors had to apply traction to pull those vertebral bodies apart so they could maintain spinal alignment, access the fractured segment, and perform the repair.

To operate on Scott's cervical spine, the doctors preferred to go in through the front, making a roughly four-inch incision on the left side of his neck. Although the spine runs along the back of the body, the damaged part of Scott's spine was on the part of the column that faces front. So, when the surgeons opened his neck, rather than having to cut their way through muscle to reach the inner face of his spinal column, they could push away the jungle of structures in the front of his neck—carotid artery, jugular vein, trachea, esophagus, thyroid, and the sinewy ropes of *longus coli* muscles along the side of the throat—to reach their destination.

Once inside, they removed the broken vertebral bodies and scraped out the discs—the spongy separators between the vertebrae—and then it was time to repair the bony spinal column using a graft from Scott's hip. The doctors made an incision in his right side and sawed a piece of bone off his iliac crest, the broad, bowl-like "wing" that forms the hipbone.

From the outside, bones feel like rigid, structural supports. Bone is actually miraculous, live material made up of two components—the hard, outer part called cortical bone, and the inner, spongy part, called cancellous bone. "Cancellous" is a term that refers to anything with a porous, open structure. In fact, this soft cancellous bone tissue, which we know as "marrow," looks like a honeycomb under a microscope, and is loaded with stem cells. Stem cells are pluripotential cells—they have the remarkable ability to develop into different types of tissue depending on where they are in the body, and so, in the right environment, they can make additional bone. The iliac crest has marrow that is especially rich in stem cells, so it is often doctors' first choice for bone graft material.

When the grafted material—the spongy cancellous tissue mixed with chips of cortical bone—is packed into place, it gets right to work. Assuming there is good blood supply and not too much disrupting motion, the stem cells use the matrix provided by the remaining bone and the cortical chips in the graft material to undergo a dynamic process of specialization. From day one, the stem cells start to multiply, maximizing in number in about three weeks. Then, a process of calcification begins, in which the tissue models itself into new bone with a hard outer surface and a spongy middle. In a few months, it will feel relatively solid, but it actually takes twelve to eighteen months before it is ideally structured to handle the forces that it must withstand.

To repair Scott's cervical spine, the surgeons sized and bent a titanium plate to fit smoothly over the new, cleaned-out space in his spinal column, and attached it with screws to C6 and T1—the healthy vertebrae just above and below the repair. Then, the bone graft from his hip was packed around the plate, where it would eventually form new bone and, with the plate, serve as a new protective, albeit rigid, column for Scott's neck.

When his neck structures were returned to their rightful places and the neck and hip incisions closed, the Gardner-Wells tongs were removed from Scott's head, and he was log-rolled face-down onto another table. It was time for operation number two.

Although the injury to Scott's mid-back or thoracic spine was not as acutely life-threatening, its repair was a longer and far more elaborate undertaking. This time, to access his spine, doctors were forced to enter from the back. It would have been impossible to enter through his abdomen, where a host of complex structures, including his stomach and intestines, would be in the way.

So they entered from the posterior, where they had to detach—literally cut away—the layers of densely packed muscles that are attached along the length of the spine. But that delicate and time-consuming process was actually the least of their problems. The incision that stretched roughly eight inches from his T7 to his T12 vertebrae exposed a war zone.

The subcutaneous tissue and muscle were severely swollen and bloody, and countless pieces of shattered bone that had sprayed all over were now wedged into the surrounding tissues. The surgeons first picked out those pieces, which they saved to perform a second, more extensive bone graft. But of course, those fragments would not be enough, so they made Scott's fourth incision of this very long day, to extract a sizable portion of his left iliac crest.

When the bone shrapnel was removed and the area prepared, straight rods were aligned along Scott's spine and fastened with seven screws to the T8 and T11 vertebrae—just above and below the T9 and T10 site of impact. The harvested bone from the fragments and hip was packed around the rods. Then, the doctors wrestled all of Scott's muscles back into place and reattached them along his spine.

In skill and stamina, it takes an ironman team of surgeons to perform reparations of this complexity and length. Scott's operation, like most orthopedic surgery, is not delicate work. It required continuous heavy labor of hammering, pounding, and chiseling. Add to that the rigorous, time-consuming process of preparing Scott's damaged insides for renovation, and detaching cross-hatched layers of muscles, and then, literally, tugging the muscles back into place.

Then there was the other ironman, Scott, who had now been transformed into a true man of steel. His age, health, and considerable strength were critical in helping him to survive the ordeals of an accident and a surgery that, by all rights, should have killed him. Unfortunately, there would be many more ordeals to come.

When he was wheeled out of the operating room and into the surgical intensive care unit, it was about 5:00 in the morning on May 26. Exactly twenty-four hours before, he had been giving a still-sleeping Cindy a kiss good-bye, anticipating his first cup of coffee, gearing up to get a load of timber to Glens Falls, and getting psyched about that new circle-saw. Now, he was lost in an anesthesia-induced sleep from which he would awake scared and disoriented, because, while he was out, the world had been turned upside down. This was no longer his before-life. It was his after-life.

As one physician said after reading Scott's surgical report, "The recuperative powers are incredible, but it's very, very intense surgery this guy had. The pain of recuperation and physical therapy I can only imagine." Then, he paused for a long moment before adding, "Actually... I can't imagine really."

Throughout it all—the tests, the surgery, the waiting—the Remingtons stayed put. They paced and slept and slept and paced in the waiting room, their first of many fitful nights on couches and chairs and floors. Scott's uncle Mike and aunt Linda Remington rented a room at a nearby motel—"Make it open-ended," they told the proprietor, "for as long as the family needs it."—and, after the first couple of days, everyone began taking turns using the room to wash up or catch a couple hours in a real bed.

Everyone except Renee. She refused to leave the hospital, and for the ten days that Scott was kept in ICU, she never left his bedside. "That goes back to my promise to Scott. I said, 'I won't leave until you're all right.' And I didn't."

For the entire seventeen days that Scott was in Burlington, there were always other Remingtons in Burlington, too, along with a continuous parade of extended family and friends, while back home, a community was digging deep into its hearts and pockets.

5.

A vigil tied in blue

E arle wishes he could free his mind of the accident and Scott's nearly ten-day struggle in the ICU, but the images won't go away. "I'm telling you, he was an absolute mess. There wasn't much left of him, really. It's hard to explain unless you were there to see it. That stuff never leaves your head. And people don't understand, you can do anything or try to block it out, but it's always in the back of your head."

Scott was still bloated all over, not just from the trauma, but also from lying face-down for so long in the operating room. At first, he was heavily sedated, but even when he regained consciousness, the tubes to the ventilator made it impossible to talk. After three years, his brother-in-law, John Smith, still couldn't talk about it without choking up. "Just to see him labor so… God, my voice is getting… He was just laboring so. That was something I just couldn't handle. He was trying so hard to breathe and the machines were… it was a scary sight."

At one point, Gert went in to see her boy, and, though he was still hooked to the ventilator, she simply couldn't get out of her mind that he had laid in the woods all alone, and she couldn't help but ask him, "Weren't you afraid that somebody wasn't going to come and find you?" With his finger, Scott wrote on his hand, "No—faith, Dad, Earle." And it hit her: "That's why he couldn't close his eyes." Later, when the ventilator was removed, he would tell his mom, "I knew if I closed my eyes, my body would just shut down. It would have been over. I had to just fight it." That's when Gert realized, "He had a lot more faith than I ever thought he did. I think he is very strong spiritually, even though he never let on. He fought to live."

The family camped out in the waiting room for the entire first three days, seeing him every chance they could. Then, little by little, they began using the motel room in tag-team fashion. During Scott's first night in ICU, when Cindy ran home to reassure the children, Renee dragged a recliner up to his bedside and held his hand all night long. "Every hour on the hour, he would squeeze my hand and I remember saying, 'You're OK, you're OK. You're still with us.'"

That initial post-op period "was so draining," says Denise, "but Renee would not leave his side, so we took turns. We couldn't leave her there. All we could think was, if something happens to Scott, she can't be there alone. So, we took turns staying with her at night."

Eventually, there was a steady back and forth flow between home and hospital.

Stephanie and Keith got into a rhythm of staying at the hospital until late at night, then going home to sleep with their children and heading back to Vermont by about seven each morning. Chris Johnson traveled back and forth two or three times a week. And, for most of the first week, Denise's husband, Bill, was simply driven by nerves: "About four nights in a row, I'd leave about ten, eleven o'clock at night, and come back home and talk to the kids. I might sit and rest for an hour or so in my chair, and then turn around and go back to the hospital."

Relatives and friends came one after the other to hold Scott's hand and hug the family. Scott's surgery began on a Tuesday and ended Wednesday morning. Chris and Ed Jay left the children with Cindy's mom, and came to see Scott that first weekend. It tore them up inside. "I had nightmares after," says Chris. "It didn't look like him, and the respirator was just very scary—the noise. But the one thing that keeps coming to mind is, I went in and was talking to Scott, and I told him that the kids were doing great, and I was keeping them safe. And he took his finger and wrote the letters t-h-a-n-k-s in my hand. It was incredible." Ed was equally stunned and moved: "You have to consider that Scott was always a very active, healthy kind of guy when this happened. And to see him paralyzed with all these tubes and everything coming out of him... I remember wholeheartedly to this day, and I'll never forget him communicating by spelling the letters of 'thanks' in the palm of our hands for taking care of his kids. It gets my throat going to this day."

Scott's friend since the fifth grade, Jim Peck, took off from work the day after he heard about the accident, and went to Burlington. "They let me in to see him, even though we're just close friends. Just his family was supposed to be in there. But they let me in, and truthfully, I didn't think he was going to live. His face was all bloated and his arms,

I mean everything. They had him on all sorts of machines and a breathing tube. He just didn't look like the same person. He wasn't able to talk, but he'd just grab hold of my hand and squeeze it."

After several days, Wendy and Ted Meade came with Randy Dooris. "We were very nervous," Wendy admits. "I remember Randy standing in the background with tears freely coming out of his eyes. We were all just nervous, we didn't know what to say or what to do. So we all just went in and were ourselves, I guess." Ted remembers that "there were a lot of people there, and we didn't have much time," but they can still envision Scott signing, "I can't move my legs."

Unfortunately, Earle was forced to make one trip home that was like tearing the scab off a wound. It was bad enough that he had to arrange to get all the equipment— skidders, saws, pulp truck, loader—back to Scott's garage. Having been an eyewitness—perhaps the most important eyewitness—to Scott's accident, he also had to go back to rehash every detail of that day with the insurance investigators. He knew full well how rough it would be, and he dreaded it. "I had to do that before, for my friend, Roger. With Scott, I was the one there and the one who had seen everything, so I had to go through all that. It wasn't easy."

Earle left for Brant Lake, but, back at the hospital, Cindy was worried about him and asked Denise's husband, Bill, if he'd go back and help Earle get through it. Bill is insured through the same company and is familiar with the agents who cover the area. Bill left Burlington about

4:00 in the morning to meet Earle by 6:00, so they could go to the site together.

The accident was barely two days old when Earle, Bill, and foresters Ray Saladin and Johnny Pratte gathered at the site with the insurance investigators and a couple of state police officers.

"It's just like on TV," Earle explains. "They draw the chalk line where the body was—how he laid there, how the arms were, how the legs were." And there were a million questions. Did you touch him? Did you try to carry him? "I said, 'No, no, no, no!' And of course, I'm glad I did, or he probably wouldn't have use of his arms today."

Bill remembers how very long a day it was. They were in the woods maybe five hours, speculating on every detail, "trying to put things together, because, of course, nobody was really going to know, except Scott." Earle could only handle the day in spurts. The men could see the actual imprint in the ground where Scott lay, and Earle found that he just had to get out of there sometimes. "He went back and forth to the header," says Bill. "He was still shaky."

Earle stopped at his parents' house before heading back to Vermont, and gathered clothes, shampoo, toothpaste, and "just stuff to freshen up with," because back in Burlington, they—and Scott, of course—were in for a long haul.

Under the circumstances, thank goodness for a little brainstorm from Gert.

Scott was suffering physically and emotionally, and everyone was trying to figure out how to raise his spirits. The family was gathered in the waiting room, when Gert turned to Renee and said, "Let's find out what Scott's favorite color is." He told them, blue. So, Gert convinced the family that they should wear little blue ribbons in his honor and give blue ribbons to everyone who came to visit. They discussed it amongst themselves and agreed to find a store and buy a skein of ribbon, some shears, and safety pins.

Later that day, they walked over to the elevator to grab a bite to eat in the cafeteria, and, when the doors opened, they ran into another family that had been marking time with them in the waiting room. Gert laughs, remembering that when the elevator doors opened, the other family "instantly put their hands over their chests, and we couldn't figure out why." The folks in the elevator couldn't keep straight faces for long, and when they took their hands away, not only were they all wearing blue ribbons, but they had just returned from buying a big roll of blue ribbon and safety pins for their new friends. "These were perfect strangers," marvels Gert, "but they ended up being family in the end. We sat up there in the waiting room and cut up ribbon, and anybody who came to visit, we gave them blue ribbons to wear in support of Scott."

With the steady traffic of well-wishers, blue ribbons began showing up on lapels around town. Then Renee called one of her best friends, Ellen McDermott, who owned a flower shop in Chestertown at the time. Ellen remembers Renee saying, "'Put blue ribbons up all over town!' So I did. I put big bows around the telephone poles up and down the streets." But she never dreamed the idea would catch fire, and that the fire would be so hot.

Ellen began giving little blue bows away at her shop in exchange for donations, and before she knew it, "everybody found out. I just couldn't believe the ribbons that I was making. Every five minutes, people came in and said, 'Are you making ribbons?' I was making those ribbons left and right."

Roger Daby also began handing out ribbons for donations at his general store in the center of Brant Lake. He had collected money at the store in the past for a number of other causes, but this was on another level. "More elaborate," he says. "There were so many people involved, and it was such a tragic thing."

At the annual Memorial Day Parade, within days of the accident, "word got back to us," says Gert, "that all the firemen and the ladies' auxiliary and all the fire trucks in the parade were covered with blue ribbons. I'm telling you that would make anybody cry. I mean I heard it, and I couldn't believe it."

The parade was the tip of the iceberg. Friends, neighbors, and "perfect" strangers covered all three towns—Brant Lake, Chestertown, and Pottersville—with blue ribbons—mailboxes, doors, light posts, signs, anyplace anybody could tie a bow.

And jars appeared on countertops in stores, the library, restaurants, public buildings. Little jars everywhere, gathering loose change for Scott and Cindy. An appeal went out in the newspaper for donations to help the family, and, later that summer, the Brant Lake Association put together the Scott Remington Invitational Golf Tournament at Cronin's Golf Course.

When all was said and done, the community sent Scott enough get-well cards to fill a lineup of shopping bags, and Cindy got a bankbook with $28,494.

Every card, every dollar, every ribbon, every visitor's touch formed a link in an emotional scaffold that bolstered the family and held Scott up when he felt like crumbling.

Living in a small town is "like that TV show *Cheers*," says Ellen. "Everybody knows your name." Sometimes that can be good and sometimes it can be not-so-good. News travels fast. "But this was a good time. Something to be proud of. When the shit hit the fan, everybody came together. Everybody came together and helped with food and money and babysitting and dog watching, it was phenomenal."

Bull was born and bred in Brant Lake. Gert grew up in Bolton Landing, the next town over, and came to live in Brant Lake when she and Bull married. And still, people surprised them. "One thing I will say about my children, and I don't mean to brag," says Gert, "I'm very proud of them. Do you know that not one of them worried whether they'd have a job or not. They stayed in Vermont for many days around the clock. They all told their bosses that family came first. And that meant so much to me. You wonder when you bring your children up just how much you instill in them. And they said their family was most important. And then with our town, I'll tell you we had moral support like no tomorrow. You just can't imagine. It just made me cry. Just knowing how people showed their love."

The town's love may have taken her aback, but the way her kids came through should have come as no surprise at all. Gert and Bull had long since laid a foundation that made it obvious to everyone that, as one neighbor put it, "Those Remingtons are a special bunch."

6.

Sealed with a KISS

Ask Gert, "So what kind of a kid was Scott growing up?"

"Brat!" she'll tell you. "Well, he was my youngest, and when they'd play ball, he had to have more than three outs. But he was a good kid."

Ask Denise: "He's always been the brat. Y'know he was a soccer star in high school. Just always got his own way."

And Renee: "We called him 'the brat.' We still call him that. When he was young, he got away with everything because he was the baby. But no, he was a good kid, we just thought he got away with more."

Scott pretty much shrugs it off. "I've got one brother and three sisters. They all call me the brat for some reason."

Gert and Bull had Denise, then Earle two years later, then three years later came Steph, two years later Renee, and the next year, Scott. He was the youngest in a family

63

that eventually had seven snowmobiles parked in the driveway. They were a family constantly on the move—hunting, snowmobiling, camping, hiking, *and* working. Nearly every weekend, the brood would trek five to six miles through the woods, and Scott was pulled along for all of it just as soon as he could keep up.

Gert has always been a huge believer in togetherness. Every summer when the kids were young, she'd take them up to Lake Minerva when school got out. Bull, who ran a business with his brother, Jim, at the time, hauling and laying gravel, came up after work when he could and on the weekends. "We just tented it," says Steph, "big, old canvas tents, not like the ones they have today." Gert and Bull slept in one, the kids piled into the other, and Steph remembers those days as happy, carefree times, even though being the middle kid meant, "I always got stuck with the two younger ones. Always! It seems like I never got to the point where I could do anything with the older kids. But, hey, we had a good time."

They slept in those tents on cots, and cooked out all summer long. Scott had a couple of aunts and uncles and cousins up at the lake, too, and everyone just played and played all summer. "They had tennis, basketball, a lake to swim in with a rope to jump off," says Scott. "There were just lots of families hanging out. That was a lot of fun." And it was during one of those summers—no one can recall the year—when someone started calling him "Goober." It started as a goof, but the damn name stuck, and they use it to this day.

That was just the way Gert wanted it. When her children were young, family life—like summers at the lake—was about fun and harmony. Except maybe for that one time when Renee got ticked off at some little girl and whacked her with a tennis racket. But fun is exactly how Scott's cousin, Bud DeMatties, whose mother is Gert's sister, remembers those summers, when his family would set up camp right next to the Remingtons.

Bud was Renee's age, and, since "she was kind of a tomboy when she was younger," he says, "she would hang out with Scott and me and Scott's other cousin, Jimmy Remington, all the time. We were basically like Huck Finn guys all the time—didn't wear shoes all summer—and we did everything together, normal boy stuff, messing around at lakeside, jumping off ropes into the water."

When the boys were teenagers and they no longer went to the lake, Bud started spending a couple of weeks during the summer at Aunt Gert and Uncle Bull's. Bud and Scott were as close as brothers, and their personalities made a powerful combination. "We grew up hunting and fishing together, and that was a lot of bonding time," says Bud. "We're a lot alike. We have the type of personality that can be good or bad I guess, because we don't have a lot of fear. We're both kind of go-all-out people. That could be bad if you went into drugs and stuff like that, but neither of us really did." Still, he admits, "when we were growing up, I think it was difficult at times for our families."

If the boys went snowmobiling, "we went *riding!*" says Bud. They often came home with a wrecked machine, or "we may have to work on one of the snowmobiles when we got back, because it wouldn't be in such good shape." And it was Bud, along with Jimmy and another cousin, Bruce, who was in the Jeep when Scott rolled it down Hickory Hill Mountain. Jimmy was able to jump out, but Scott, Bruce, and Bud were all thrown out. The vehicle rolled right over Bud, and he knows it was a miracle he survived. Jimmy took off down the mountain after the Jeep, actually caught it in motion, and was able to stop it just before it slammed into a pine tree. Scott just shakes his head in disbelief at the memory: "There wasn't one straight piece of metal on the thing. That was *definitely* one of my nine lives."

It all sounds so reckless, says Bud, "but that was the funny thing." They were never out to deliberately hurt themselves or anyone else, they were never violent or destructive, and they never went crazy with alcohol. "Even when we were teenagers," says Bud, "if we were drinking we weren't driving. We were probably just hanging out at our own house." It was just that, when it came to anything physical, they pushed the limits, and, Bud is convinced that, "That ended up being a lifesaver for Scott. He never had any limitations set for himself. I really believe that was a lot of what actually gave him the ability to survive his accident."

If family was about fun, it was also about responsibility. Every week, Gert marched all five kids off to Sunday school and church. "Dad didn't always go," says Steph, "but Mom did," and there was no acting up. "With five kids in one pew, oh we'd be in trouble. She had to split us up all the time, especially when we made my dad's sister laugh. And my grandmother would get so mad, too, and say, 'You're old enough, you're not supposed to be laughing!'"

Everybody also knew from an early age that he or she would be expected to work, no excuses. Gert made the girls baby-sit and clean the house, and, "when we were old enough, about thirteen," says Steph, "Mom made us all get jobs." In the winter, when Bull made extra money plowing driveways, Gert always assigned one of the kids to go with him so he wouldn't fall asleep. "That was kind of hard on us," says Steph, "because the next day we'd have to go to school." But she and Scott and the rest of the kids hold warm and vivid memories of being out in the truck with Bull late at night doing driveways. He'd visit with a number of his customers, who often invited him and his co-pilot in for coffee and maybe a little something to eat. "I remember doing the plowing a lot with him," says Scott. "We'd go to the diner in the middle of the night—one, two o'clock in the morning—and have a cheeseburger."

Bull also taught Earle and Scott to drive as soon as they could reach the pedals and see over the dashboard in his pickup. He'd take them out to the sandpits near their home and teach them the finer points of operating vehicles and other types of equipment. Scott was too young to help much in the gravel business, but he used to ride a lot with his dad in the truck, and his dad and Uncle Jim taught him how to run the bulldozer. And from time to time, "I'd sleep in the dump truck when they drove the gravel," he remembers. "They didn't know how I did it, but I'd sleep there."

Then, when Bull and Jim went into logging, the boys became loggers, too, and they pulled their weight alongside the men. That included putting up with the inherent dangers of the job.

It's the rare logger who hasn't had his share of injuries, and Earle and Scott were no exceptions. Gert raced Earle to the hospital once when he nearly took off his kneecap with a chainsaw, and Scott cut his finger and the back of his leg when he tripped and fell on his still-running saw. During the summers that Bud came to stay with the Remingtons, he went out logging, too. "We used to run the chainsaws," says Scott, "probably weren't supposed to—I've got the cuts to show all over my body. But my dad and uncle taught us to do different stuff and run the loader. My cousin, Rusty, used to come and help, too, sometimes. That's back when we used to handle a lot of the wood with a pulp hook, and we had to cut it all in four-foot lengths."

From those experiences and from the cuts and sweat, Scott soaked up his father's powerful work ethic, learned that business is about honesty and reliability, and internalized the nature of wood.

"He just doesn't slack," says his boyhood friend, Bill Strauss, who moved to Brant Lake in the ninth grade. "I met him when I was fourteen years old, and after school and on weekends, he was working in the family business. He's not afraid to get his hands dirty. He's a great person— he doesn't pull punches, and tells it like it is."

Thinking back, Scott chooses his words carefully as he tries to explain what it is about working, playing, and just being around wood. "There's something in you that just knows. I was good at it. I just know the smell of the wood. Y'know, I could go into the woods and tell you any tree, and I could just look at it and tell you how much money you'd make off it."

The woods became even more of a comfort zone for Scott, when he was about thirteen, and Bull began to pass on his reverence for "the season." Hunting season in the Adirondacks runs from late October to early December, and, for the Remington men and most of their friends and relatives, life took on a singular focus during those months. Before Scott and Earle were old enough for their own hunting licenses, Bull would bring them along with their uncles and friends, like Bryce Johnson. "As the boys came along, they just joined in the party," says Bryce, "and we spent a lot of years together."

With their work and other responsibilities, most of the men didn't get a lot of time to be together during the rest of the year, but, come October, "it was our time," says Bryce. "It was just enjoyable to be with a bunch of guys out in the woods, and we all had a good time." For the most part, they would take day trips, leaving at the crack of dawn and coming back after dark. But at least once during the season, they'd all head north to Pharaoh Lake, and "spend a week in there and hunt and camp and just kind of get together and have a great time."

Scott incorporated the season into the rhythm of his own life as he grew older and later, after he got married. It was just a guarantee that weekend days during that roughly two-month stretch were about being in the woods with the guys, bagging deer if you were lucky, getting back together a few days later to drink beers and butcher the kill, and filling the freezer with fresh meat. From his dad and uncle and family friends, Scott learned how to gut a deer in the woods before hauling it home, where they would hang it up for a few days before butchering.

After Scott bought his dad's logging business, he and his friends would hang their kill on a post that jutted out along the side of the garage where Scott kept his equipment. "Sometimes there'd be six or seven bucks hanging out there," he says. The garage is right on the side of the main road heading into Brant Lake, and Scott and the guys would crack up when they heard people "slam on their brakes" seeing those carcasses dangling from the garage, which Jimmy had decorated with the racks (antlers) from previous kills. Sometime during the week following a hunt, the guys would set up a big table at the garage, have a few beers, and spend the evening skinning and butchering their game. It's hard work, but "you just relax and do it," says Scott. "It was fun, you'd just be with your friends."

There's just something about it, says Scott's friend Bill Lajeunesse. Bill is old enough to be Scott's dad—his daughter-in-law, Karen, is Renee's best friend—but he did a lot of hunting and camping and "running around on ATVs" with Scott.

"The guys used to build their own hunting camp back in the woods," Bill explains, "and it would stay up through the whole hunting season. They'd put it up out of small sapling trees, make a frame, throw tarps over it, and bring in a wood stove. Then they'd string up gas lights with rubber hose all around the ceiling, and you could sit in there with a T-shirt on, no matter how cold it is, with the wood stove going, and the place would be warm." The guys dubbed it "the blue room," because the tarps they used, which were blue, were bright in the daylight and aglow at night from the gas lights and stove. "You just talk about all the good times, the things you're gonna do," says Bill. "You plan for the hunt the next day, your strategy and all that, and you eat well and you're with your friends. You hope you get something the next day, and if you don't, who cares? You still had a good day."

And according to Bill, you never take just anybody into your camp. He's been hunting for more than forty years, and people ask him all the time if they can go along, but he almost always says no. "You don't always know how they are," he says without a hint of apology. "People can't just say, 'Hey, can I come?' I don't know if my friends will like them. I don't know how they hunt. You have to be a certain person to get into a hunting camp. When you're invited to go to somebody's hunting camp, it's an honor and a privilege."

As a kid, when Scott wasn't working or hunting, or fighting to stay awake in class, he was riding bikes all over hell and gone with Chris Johnson, playing soccer and basketball, and just hanging with his best friends, who included his cousins and his sister, Renee.

"Scott and I were four and five in the lineup," says Renee. "We were always close, I mean from day one." When Scott was in fifth grade and Renee was in sixth, their oldest sister, Denise, who was eighteen, got married, and the next year, Earle married. So, circumstances just kept drawing them closer and closer.

When the two hit high school, and especially after Steph graduated, they were inseparable. "We did everything together," Renee remembers. "We were both into sports. He did soccer, I played field hockey, so we hung out with a lot of the same people. If we went to a bonfire on a Friday night, we were both at the same place. And every winter, Saturday mornings, Mom knew that there goes Scott and Renee on the snowmobiles, and we had to be back by dinnertime. And I can remember going in his room all the time and flopping on his bed, listening to KISS and that song, *Beth*, and talking about school and this and that."

That wasn't the half of it. When Renee wanted to start dating, Gert told her, "Okay, you can go, but only if Scott's with you." "So here would be my boyfriends or John, who I married, going somewhere, and there would be Scott sitting in the back seat! It was funny. In the beginning, my husband was like, 'Jeez, Scott, he's so annoying!'" And whenever Renee would bring a boy home for dinner, it wasn't too long before he was outside shooting hoops with Scott.

Through chemistry and accidents of birth, Renee and Scott were joined at the hip, but Gert wasn't about to let the bonds among all her children fade, just because life was taking them in different directions. Denise's first husband, Kevin, was in the navy, and wherever they were stationed, the family went to visit. When Kevin was based in California, Gert scraped the money together and left with the family on a Thursday and came home on Monday, "just to see her and make sure she was all right," says Steph.

Another time, Gert packed all the kids into the station wagon and drove to Mississippi to spend a week with Denise. After Steph left for college, Denise, Kevin, and their children, Miranda and Christopher, were reassigned to Hawaii, where Denise gave birth to twins, Jeffrey and Jeremy, and Gert was not about to be held back by the Pacific Ocean. She announced to the family that they couldn't afford to see Denise *and* buy Christmas presents that year, so, if everybody agreed, Hawaii would be their present. They agreed.

"We were just always together," says Steph. "When we went to bed, we always said good night to our parents, and we always told them we loved them. My mother always came in and said, 'Good night,' and they always said, 'I love you.'"

Funny how things work out. Gert and Bull, like all parents, raised their family by the seats of their pants. Who could have guessed that loading the clan in the wagon time after time to make sure Denise was all right, and piling the kids into a canvas tent summer after summer, where they were packed in so close they could reach out in the night and give each other a pinch, would come in so handy? Perfect boot camp for the trials ahead.

7.

A squeeze and a wink

For the nearly ten days that Scott spent in the surgical intensive care unit, he and everyone he cared about occupied parallel universes. Scott was in solitary confinement on one side of a divide, while his family and friends waited and worried on the other. Just as when Earle and forester Johnny Pratte stayed with Scott in the woods during the interminable moments after the accident and before help arrived, his loved ones were always close enough to touch and yet miles away. Once again, Scott found himself alone but not alone.

Nothing presents a more stark illustration of this psychic separation than the juxtaposition of Scott's daily hospital records and the journal that his family faithfully kept throughout his hospital stay. Their written thoughts, especially during his days in ICU, are particularly poignant. Scott was amazed when he finally read the journal months later, and discovered what everyone around him had been thinking and doing and saying while he was lost to painkillers or to pain that refused to bow to medication.

<u>May 26</u>

Patient in need of prophylactic IVC [inferior vena cava] filter following multiple trauma. The patient was informed of the risks of the procedure and written consent obtained. Conscious sedation was administered with monitoring of heart rate, blood pressure and respiratory rate.

(Scott had been wheeled into the ICU early in the morning on the 26th. He received four units of blood and appeared to be in stable condition. However, given his paralysis, doctors were worried that he might develop an embolus, or blood clot, in one of his legs, which could potentially travel up through his *inferior vena cava* to his heart and lungs. Like tributaries emptying into a river, veins running up the legs and lower torso merge about bellybutton-level into one giant vein called the *vena cava*, which sends blood into the right atrium of the heart, where it is quickly pumped to the lungs. "Inferior" simply refers to the portion of the *vena cava* that is below the heart, whereas the "superior" *vena cava* is the portion above.

If Scott's body sent a blood clot into his lungs, it would be fatal.

Scott was in danger of developing a "pulmonary embolus," literally a "lung clot," for a couple of reasons. He could no longer move his legs, which meant that he was no longer making the voluntary and involuntary movements that continually keep blood flowing through the vascular system. In addition, his body, which was in the throes of trauma from the fractures and tissue damage, was actively producing the proteins that encourage clotting. As a result, there was a danger that blood would pool in his lower extremities and eventually form a clot, and that a piece of the clot would break off and travel through his bloodstream.

To prevent such an embolus from traveling up from his legs to his lungs, doctors needed to insert a filter in his *vena cava* to stop any potential clot in its tracks.

So, on May 26, literally hours after his surgery, Scott was back in the operating room, under conscious sedation, where his right groin was prepped and draped. A needle was inserted into the vein in his right thigh. A wire was passed through the needle and snaked up through his leg to just above the level of his kidneys. Then a tiny "over-the-wire Greenfield filter" was positioned in his *vena cava* where it would stand sentry, ready to catch clots for the rest of his life.

Scott was also fitted that day for the hard neck brace and plastic body jacket that would be strapped around him to encase his torso. For months to come, he would not be allowed to sit up without first being strapped into the collar and body jacket.)

Wednesday 26th - Snack basket from Meads, Griffens, Meades & McDermotts. Gallo Realty 4 pizzas. Renee

<u>May 27</u>
Tube feedings were advanced to full rate and tolerated well. Patient remained on the ventilator due to "paradoxical movement of his sternum."

(In other words, Scott was unable to breathe on his own, not only because of his punctured right lung, but also because, instead of his chest moving in normal rhythmic fashion with every breath—out as he inhaled and in as he exhaled—his broken sternum and ribs moved "paradoxically." As one doctor described it, the sternum, as well as the ribs that should have been anchored to the sternum, were "flailed" or free-swinging—moving in as he inhaled and out as he exhaled.)

Hi Scott, I love you too much. I praise God for sending his angels over you. You are alive… I pray that your body will heal quickly and that your pain will soon ease up somewhat. Mom

A wonderful night last night with you - I held your hand and waited for your squeeze. Once every hour you squeezed. We made it through. Renee

Blue ribbons on their way!!! Aunt Linda called this pm. Went home last night! Was not an easy decision to leave but will stay for a bit now! John & Jenna love you very much! Sis says she wants her daddy home - NOW! Aunt Gay called this pm. Ted called tonight! Cindy

May 28

An attempt was made to wean from vent and Pt [patient] was extubated. He was found to be alert and appropriate.

(Around 5:00 in the evening, the ventilator tube that went through Scott's nose and down into his throat was pulled out.)

Scott, we got our blue ribbon on for you. We are all praying for you. We love you. Uncle Rusty called this morning. Love, Aunt Jackie

Scott, we're here rooting for you. We know you're on the mend. We love you. Everything will work out. You're too important to us to allow anything to happen to you. You're a trooper. You will make it. We're here counting on you. Love, Aunt Lulu

Hey Uncle Scott. I'm glad you are still around. Somebody to be around to joke with. I'll have to wait until you get better to play hoops. I leave in August to go to Texas. Then I'll be back to visit you. Well take care and just remember I'm here for you and I love you. Love, Miranda

Hey Uncle Scott. Hope you're feeling better. Really hoping you get better real fast. We'll pull through this together. We're all pulling for you. I will be here for you. I love you. Love Jeff

Uncle Scott I hope you're feeling better. We are all wearing our blue ribbons thinking of you… Just remember we love you. Love Jeremy

Hi Scott, Hope you are feeling better. I am thinking of you all the time. I am praying for you too. If you ever need to talk, anytime, Goob just call. If you need anything, just ask. Love, Keith

Goober - Surely wish we were out and about, having some Labatts Blue! Keep up the good work.. We are all behind you 110%, now and always. Love John [Renee's husband]

You are improving each day and bring such joy to our hearts. Truly you are a miracle and I am so thankful we still have you. My love always, Renee

Hi Scott so glad that I was able to stay at the hospital last night with Cindy. Snuck down a couple of times in the night to check on you… I enjoy it every time you look at me and wink at me and tell me that you love me. Isabelle Carpenter sent a beautiful card to me by Keith along with $300.00. I gave it to Cindy as I feel that you could use it to cover some of your expenses. It makes me feel good to hear about all of the prayers and support we're getting from our family and friends. Pastor Brett called again last night. He will be calling again tonight…I wish I could take your pain away from you and hear your voice. Wish they would let us spend more time with you. Love you too much, mom

Hey babe! My love for you is unconditional! No matter what the outcome - I'll always be here and I will always love you! Be patient. Good things come to those who wait! I really believe you are in the best of care here at Fletcher Allen. Time will be a major factor! This will be a long haul - but I am here for the heavy load! I love you always and forever! Cindy

Scott, Believe it or not I am cheering for Jeff Gordon just for you. Hang in there. I love you. Love Aunt Jackie.

5 p.m. Scott so happy we have had an answer to prayer. Your respirator has just been taken out and it was so good to come in and see a smile on your face. Earle, Bill & Denise are going to spend the night with us tonight. I feel so proud that we have such a close knit family. So glad that you have taken another step in your recovery. You'll have many, many more steps you'll have to take on the road to recovery and probably a few hills to climb. But I know you can do it. Love you too much, mom

Dear Scott, It's Friday 5/28 - we arrived here at the hospital about 5:30 PM after being lost for a while - thought I knew where I was going - oh- well! John & Jenna were so good on the trip over - we stopped and got them food at McDonald's so they would be OK for a while. Anxious to see how you are doing now that your tube is out. Ann & Jim send their love and prayers. Shel & Sara also want you to know that they love you and send their best wishes. You have no idea how many people have been calling and offering their help. Uncle Jim has been a mess but will feel better when he sees you and knows you're OK. Love, Aunt Cil

<u>May 29</u>

Afternoon Pt was nasally reintubated secondary to ABG's [arterial blood gases—measured to determine the amount of oxygen and carbon dioxide dissolved in the blood] with decreasing pO_2 and rising pCO_2.

(Scott's baby step forward was short-lived. Doctors detected decreasing oxygen and rising carbon dioxide in his system. X-rays revealed that the right lung "remains virtually opacified." That is, on the X-ray, Scott's lung showed up white; a healthy lung shows up black. The puncture had not yet healed, and, since his chest was still full of blood, he drew fluid into the lung with every breath. What's more, with the fractured sternum, he simply didn't have the strength to exchange enough gases in and out. He had to be re-intubated.)

Day #5 - A good start - you told me I needed a shower! You're right and when the rest of the family arrives we'll go back to the hotel and get cleaned up. John, Earle and I spent the night here with you. I got some sleep (4 1/2 hrs) and so did John but Earle spent the night meeting new & strange people... Joss just arrived and here comes the family. We are so happy, actually elated you are doing so well. Midnight - 3 am rough time for you - you needed to go "poo". Why don't you just go - don't worry about it everyone goes. They gave you blood this a.m.,.. Love ya always, Renee

Scott, hi! It is 8:05 and we just got to the hospital. They told us we can't see you until 8:30. Cindy spent the nite in our room and she and I didn't get much sleep. I guess mom and I have hospital duty tonite so Renee and John can get some rest. Well Goob, I guess I am going to get another cup of coffee... We really love you and can't wait until you can go home with us... Love you lots, Denise

Good morning Scott. We had a restful night at the motel. They are wonderful over there to us. We have our rooms for as long as we need them. I am on hospital duty tonight with Denise. So glad it will be my turn to be close to you for the night... I wish I could take your pain from you... Earle is here to give you love & support also. Martin called. Joan and him are on their way over... Dakota told Steph that she wished that Uncle Earle didn't tell me that Uncle Scott was hurt and in the hospital. It's a warm sunny day. I'll be here until the day you come home from the hospital. Scott we're so proud of you. You're fighting so hard to get well. Just try to remember that there is a rainbow after the storm. Love you too much, mom

1:05 pm Hi Scott! Steph and I arrived here at 11:00 am this morning... I think you are doing great. We have been getting a lot of phone calls from your friends. We are returning them and letting them know that you are doing great. Don't worry about your lawn and "Bear" [Scott's dog]. I will mow it. Bear's in good hands... Well I gotta go for now Goob, Steph wants to go to Wal-Mart for 'women's personals' if you know what I mean! I am praying for you. Catch ya later. Love, Keith

It's 6:21 PM. I am thinking of you everyday and hope that you will get and feel better soon! I am glad that you can speak a little bit it's nice to hear your voice once in a while. You are a great uncle. You will get through this and we all are here with you to support you. We all love you very much... Write you later, OK! Bye. Love Joss You will make it through this, you will!

Scott, we all love you. We're all praying for you. I'm confident that you'll be strong enough to make a good recovery. There are many things you'll be able to do and don't forget the kids need their dad. I'll bet Uncle Bud and Grandma are watching & putting in a good word for you. Love Aunt Gay

Goob it is still the same day and John & Joss and I are the only ones in the waiting room. You are back on the respirator and resting so we can't get in to see you. Chris, Renee and Dad have gone down for a smoke and mom is in your room sitting with you... Dad was gonna go home tonite with Bill but has decided to stay. Earle just called and as soon as Pooch gets home they are coming back. He is really worried about you and feels the need to be here... Love Denise

9:30 pm. Rough PM today! Blood pressure a little low - they are going to give you more blood! Cindy

10:30 PM. Scott it's me again. I spent a good deal of the afternoon and evening with you. It breaks my heart to see you so sick, I am sorry for crying but I love you so much it hurts. I'm spending the night at the hospital tonight. I have two chairs put together for my bed. I am sorry they had to put the ventilator back in again. But if it means you'll heal quicker and keep you from getting pneumonia I can deal with it. It really upset Grandpa Barnes to see you so sick. Jennifer says she is running in a spinal injury marathon on Monday. Tim Remington called and said that they are praying for you also. I told him about the Blue Ribbons. He said that they would get some and wear them and put them on their mailboxes also. He also is getting some Jeff Gordon merchandise together and sending it up to you. Earle & Pooch are also here to spend the night tonight. Dad broke down and cried today. It upset him when he knew you had to be hooked up to the ventilator again. Cindy just came out and said your heart rate has gone down. That is a plus.... Praying that in the morning we'll see an improvement once again. Duane Bolton's wife just stopped in and said hi… Goodnight. I'll see you sometime during the night. Love you too much, mom

Goob - Rough day but tomorrow will be here soon! (11:45 pm). I sit and wonder what the future holds, if only we had a looking glass!! I'm so worried about you and only wish there was something I could do to make things better. You have a slight fever 100 and I'm anxiously awaiting your next reading. When, when - I just wish I knew when you're going to be in the clear. I love you dearly, but you already know that! You're in my every thought and prayer. Renee

<u>May 30</u>
Patient was stable, spine continued to follow.

(Stable perhaps, but Scott was struggling to tolerate the routine torture that occurred every twenty minutes or so when a nurse would turn him on his side to stave off bedsores. In a body full of broken ribs, no painkiller is a match for that. With the ventilator and feeding tubes in his nose and the chest tube on one side, Scott struggled to communicate by writing on a little memo board, but some of the staff just didn't get it. On this day, Scott remembers that things came to a head.

"I tried to tell this one guy, 'You can't roll me on my left side!' But he rolled me on my left side." Pain shot through him. "Everything was just floating in there, and it must have hit something, because they had to slit me on my other side and stick another chest tube in!" According to Renee, "He ended up having to get a second chest tube, because so much blood had pooled inside his body when they put him on his left side, which was the most severely hurt.")

2:45 AM. Good morning Scott. I pray that today we'll see a glimmer of hope and improvement in you. I was down at 1:30 to check on you. You seemed to be resting so I didn't disturb you. Renee is sleeping on the couch beside me. Denise is curled up in two chairs across the room. Earle & Pooch are on the floor in front of me. I have been praying for you as I can't sleep with the light on. Maybe the Lord feels that you need my prayers more than I need the sleep. Don't laugh but I just finished the rest of the seafood salad that Mel gave us. When I'm upset I have a tendency to eat. I love you Scott and I feel that you realize how much Dad & I love you... I got to see you at 7 this morning. Good to see you smiling once again. I'm drinking some coffee now trying hard to wake up. Aunt Cil called this morning. Cindy is now talking to Keith. Mom

11:45 am. Hey Scott - It's Kim. I had to let you know Kevin & I are here again - & of course I have to pick on you about the race that's on tonight. My guy Bobby LaBonte has pole tonight! I'm going to tape it for you - Kevin & I have thought about you so much! The girls are thinking about you too - Sierra told us she wants to take you to the circus when you are feeling better!... You'll get through this! Love ya, Kim

Scott, we made it over around 12 noon. Uncle Mike was the backseat driver for Aunt Linda... we all are here supporting you honey. Aunt Jackie

Hi Scott, Christopher and I made it up here about 10 am... About 12:15 we both finally got a chance to see you. You were still sleeping because of all the pain medication but when Christopher talked to you, you knew he was there and grabbed his hand!… Love, Brooke

Uncle Scott, I know that right now it is tough for you. It was tough for me when I was in the hospital. But I made it. Why? Because everybody was helping me out. I will always be there to help because you helped me… I'm going to try and move out to Colorado in the Fall with Brooke. So when hunting season comes out there you should fly out and we'll go hunting. You will make it. I believe… I love you. Love, Christopher

Hi it's me again Joss. I finally got to see you this afternoon at 3:45 pm. You were sleeping though… We all can't wait until you get home… Mom is now sitting in with you, you're sleeping. She thought that you were alone! <u>LOVE YOU UNCLE SCOTT</u>! Love Joss

Hi Scott! I got in to see you first thing today (Sunday). Boy, it sure is hot outside today. We are thinking about you all the time. Also, we are praying for you, Goober. Dakota is here with us today. She says Hi Uncle Scott, I love you! Adrian is home with my mom & dad. He doesn't feel very good today. I was going to mow your lawn, but Todd had already done it, also he did your father's. Catch ya later. Love, Keith

Hi Scott. It is Sunday 7:09 pm. Alice and I came over Tuesday but you were already in the op. room… How do you watch that Nascar Racing… I like it only when they crash. I hope you get out of here soon. Keep the faith. Love Ted & Alice

<u>May 31</u>

Pt had CPAP [continuous positive airway pressure] trials. Pt was febrile [feverish].

(That night, "I swore I was gonna die," says Scott. He had developed pneumonia, a common danger for someone in his condition, whose defenses are overtaxed and whose lungs are irritated and filled with fluid. In such a situation, pneumonia becomes what doctors call an "opportunistic infection"—Scott was a perfect host and the disease took advantage.

With his lungs infected, phlegm kept building up in Scott's ventilator tube, so the nurses suctioned it out at regular intervals. At one point, though, "They had just done it," he remembers, and, unable to talk, he tried to tell the nurse, using his memo pad, that, "You need to do it again!" The message didn't get through. "She thought I was just being a pain in the neck or something. I'm serious. You're lying there, you're trying to write things down, and getting frustrated, and you can't breathe! That really scared me. I was in a panic. I pointed my finger *hard* at the nurse. I remember that. So they did the suction, and good thing, because I was full.")

Good morning Scott. Cindy and I spent the night here at the hospital with you last night. I came down to check on you at 1 AM you were sleeping good. I came back down at 3 you told me you wanted me to stay with you so I came out and got Cindy for you. I felt you needed her more than me... Your white blood count isn't down too much this morning. Chris Johnson and Lynn are coming over this morning. Aunt Cil

& Uncle Jim are coming over. They're filling up the coolers with ice and soda & milk this morning. The maid cleaned the waiting room. She said the place was quite dirty. Keep up the good fight Scott, there will be better days… Mom

Scott, Things were pretty scary yesterday. But all looks well now! You had to have antibiotic in case of pneumonia… Maybe 2 or 3 more days with the ventilator! I love you lots, Cindy

Goober, Happy Memorial Day - the big parade today and you'll be represented well. You're a fighter and I know you'll keep up the fight. I wish I could make it easier for you and that's probably the most frustrating thing. We are all taking our turns sitting with you and that's a comfort to you. Sometimes small gestures are so inspiring. John just came out and said you had a scary spell - your ventilator tube was pinched and you couldn't breathe. The nurses responded immediately and corrected the problem… We are sharing in the ups and downs. We love you and always will. Renee

Hi Scott, You look better today! We are all here for you. Adrian came over today with Lori. He said Hi, and that he loves ya. We have been outside with the kids on the playground. Wow! Really hot out there. Gabby and his wife just popped in to say hi. Catch ya later, Love, Keith

Happy Memorial Day Scott. It is 5:20 pm. Denise & Bill, Cindy, Dad, John Smith, Joss-Elyse, Keith, Stephanie, Adrian, Dakota, Uncle Jim, Aunt Cil, Chris, Ed and Melissa have all gone back home. Dad & John, Keith & Stephanie will be back again in the morning. Renee & I are going to see if they'll let us *stay in your room with you tonight. So happy that they would let us all take a turn all day non-stop with you today. That sure put Joy in all of our hearts. You seem to be feeling so much better today, which makes me very happy. I took a little nap in the waiting room this afternoon as at times I get so tired I just can't hold my eyes open. I feel so much better when I am close to you. It tears me apart when the nurses tell me I can't stay as it isn't hospital policy. So many people have called and offered to do anything for any of us. It is nice to know how much everyone loves you. Love you too much, mom*

<u>June 1</u>
Cultures were sent, he was started on Amp/Gent [the antibiotics Ampicillin and Gentamicin] for broad coverage.

(Scott continued to battle infection, so more cultures were sent to the lab for analysis.)

6:50 AM. Scott I just spent the night right beside you in the recliner. It has been a week ago today since you've been hurt. You had a real bad night last night struggling to breathe. You and I slept good for one hour from 11 p.m. to midnight, the rest of the night was chaos. You told the nurse and me that you were going crazy and you would much rather die than to have to go through all of this. Scott please don't give up. Keep on fighting. I realize it is easy for me to say as I am not the one in the bed struggling to breathe. I love you Scott and I am praying for you. I'm praying that you'll be able to relax just enough so that you can get some sleep. We want them to give you something so you will sleep. You are now complaining that your chest hurts. The nurses you had before are working but on the other end of your floor. They are very concerned for you. They are also trying to get you some extra help. Everyone is on your side they all are rooting for you. I'm here in the waiting room having coffee. Renee is wandering around. It seems as though all we do is to hug each other and cry our hearts out. Scott I'm praying that today we'll have some good news… We all love you more than you can imagine. We have unconditional love for you. Earle called before 6 this morning. He is so worried about you. He told me to tell you that he loves you. mom

Goob hi! Went home last nite and came back this morning with Steph and Keith. I heard you had a rough nite last nite and we are not going to have another one like it, right? Renee and Paster Dave have gone in to see you but you said just 2 minutes. Steph and Keith and I just went down to get something to eat. You have to get well soon, we are getting real tired of the food down there… Love ya lots, Denise

Hi Scott! Hang in there Goober! Keep on fighting! We are all here for you. Steph and I will be here for you tonight and tomorrow night. Love Keith p.s. Goob, it is good to see you sitting up.

I'm back! I'm so sorry I wasn't here when things got rough last night! Unfortunately I had some things to take care of! We have 2 wonderful kids that had lots of questions & lots of tears! It was not easy to leave your side & go home. It's so hard to have to choose! They seemed to be doing better this afternoon when Gary picked them up. They are so great to take the kids. I know they are in good hands. I love you so much. Cindy

June 2
Culture showed M. Cataralis, Amp/gent were d/c'ed and Cefuroxime was started. Pt was successfully extubated and allowed up to chair in brace.

(Cultures showed that pneumonia was not the only opportunistic bug at work. With Scott unable to clear all the secretions from his lungs or to cough out the droplets of water that might gather in his breathing tube and bring along bacteria, he was a set-up for serious infection. In fact, his cultures showed the nasty Microbacterium Cataralis. The Ampicillin and Gentamicin were discontinued and Cefuroxime, a bacteria-specific antibiotic, was started.

That same day, however, was balanced by some very welcome events, indeed. The ventilator tube and both chest tubes were removed once and for all, and that evening, Scott, in neck brace and body jacket, was lifted into a chair.)

Good morning Scott. Dad, Renee & I arrived back here at the hospital at 6:30 this morning. It was good to hear that you had a good night last night. Denise, Cindy, Steph and Keith spent the night with you. Steph said you called for me in the night but you settled for her. So glad to see you were sitting up in the wheelchair last night. Also glad to know you had both chest tubes out yesterday. They're talking about taking our your ventilator this morning. Yesterday you were able to write us notes. Can't wait for you to talk with us.... mom

Hi Goob. You did great last night. Steph, myself, Cindy, Denise we all stayed here last night with you. You are looking good. I called Calvin this morning, and him and Terri are coming up to see you this weekend… 9:50 am, Cindy just came in from trying to get in to see you, but we have to wait while they get you up in the chair. She said that you're talking some too. I can't wait to hear you talk Goob… Lots of love, Keith

Dear Scott, I was in your family for 20 years and you'll always be a part of me. Stay strong and I love you. Micky

8 pm. Scott we're all very happy we've seen you up in the chair twice today. You also sat on the edge of your bed once. They have you dressed in an undershirt & shorts your glasses on. The smile on your face is so beautiful. The hug & kiss was worth a million… You are now breathing on your own… So happy to see Cody, Justin & Micky coming to visit with you. Also Aunt Jackie & Ellen… Andy Smith was so surprised how much you improved… mom

June 3
Patient was doing well off vent. Diet was advanced to full liquids. TF's [tube feedings] were continued. L wrist was X-rayed – no fractures were noted. He was transferred to the surgical floor where he continued on a smooth postoperative course.

(Although his tube feedings continued, for the first time in ten days, Scott was given liquids by mouth, and

92

finally, he was moved out of the ICU and into a regular room.)

Good news, great news, you are moving out of ICU to a regular room today. You are going to make it—what a relief. I feel like I've just received the best news I've ever had in my life! You are stuck with us! I love you so much, truly we are blessed. Love ya, Renee

Looking good Goob! Glad we had a chance to visit this morning at 5:00 AM. You were getting tired, so I left. Boy Goob, your sister likes to snore. Steph and I are going back to take a shower. Cindy & your mom got here at 7:00. Love Keith

Scott would be in the hospital for eight more days until his discharge on June 11. During that time, the list of visitors to Burlington continued to grow and grow, and the cards and other expressions of support never let up. The Remingtons stayed close and, with every jigsaw puzzle and game of catch in the waiting room, they allowed a little more tension to drain away. Every inch forward for Scott felt like victory. As Renee wrote, at one point, in the journal, "Sometimes small gestures are so inspiring."

With the whole family around to watch, Scott's feeding tube was pulled out on June 5, and little by little, the focus of each day began to shift from survival to living, beginning that day with the taste of a scrambled egg.

But the road back continued to be a bumpy one as Scott found it harder and harder to remember what it was like to cruise through a day. Pain, often searing, was constant. Given everything that his body had been through, it was those damn ribs that seemed the worst. There's really nothing that can be done for broken ribs, except to wait for them to heal on their own. Scott is emphatic when he says, "I hope I never break a rib for the rest of my life. Every breath, every movement kills."

Nothing, absolutely nothing, was easy. Food didn't even bring a respite of joy. "I just didn't feel like eating," he says. "The smell of food would make me nauseous. I would drink a lot of that iced tea—Lipton Brisk—and eat peanut M&Ms. Now I look at them and go, 'Ooo, I don't know.' I can still hear my mom—'Eat! You gotta eat.' And I'd say, 'Mom, I don't feel like it. I don't think I'm gonna fade away.'"

And then there was physical therapy, which was indescribable in his tender body. The first trick—learning to sit upright—was a trip in itself. He was not allowed to sit up without having the hard plastic brace around his body. So the nurses would roll him on his side to scoot the thing underneath him and strap it around his torso. The memory of that routine brings the pain flooding back.

Then, actually sitting required a whole new level of strength and balance. Unfortunately, his vast stores of lumberman strength were gone. After nearly two weeks lying prone, with fresh incisions in his neck and back, and with no control over his lower half and no rib cage to rely on, he had to learn from scratch. At first, he could only handle a few seconds, before waves of dizziness and rivulets of sweat pouring off his body would force his nurses to help him lie back down. After several days, though, he could sit on the edge of his bed for five to ten minutes using his hands for support. Then the therapists had him try to sit up and bat a balloon back and forth, and by June 8th, he was allowed the treat of sitting in a wheelchair, while Renee or Cindy gave him gentle rides down the halls.

It was also around this time that discussions of discharge to a rehabilitation facility began in earnest. The hospital caseworker recommended several locations, some close to home and some out of state, and the family began to weigh the pros and cons of each facility and the costs and benefits of being nearby versus far away. Cindy was lobbying to keep Scott close to home, but other family members weren't sure, and the question of insurance coverage loomed over all of their discussions—what would Scott's carrier cover, and did coverage extend out of state? Renee immediately launched a research effort, scouring the hospital's library for information, and the family attended meetings with the hospital case manager to discuss alternatives.

In Scott's mind, though, there was complete clarity. Nothing else since May 25 was so simple. Looking back over his entire hospital stay, says his sister Denise, "The only conversation I really remember with him was when he got to talking, and he just made it very clear he wanted to go to Kessler [Rehabilitation Institute in New Jersey]. He wanted to go where Christopher Reeve recuperated. He was adamant about it. We didn't know if the insurance would cover it, but he didn't care. That's where he wanted to go."

The family met again with Scott's case manager, and "we all voiced our opinion," says Denise. Scott's insistence on Kessler was on the table, but Mt. Sinai in New York

City was also a highly regarded possibility. Cindy was still concerned about making a long-term commitment to a facility that was so far away—both Kessler and Mt. Sinai were more than three hours from home. Ultimately, though, it was Scott, *in absentia*, who won out. "We just felt," says Denise, "that if he went where he felt most comfortable that things would work out better and he'd be more relaxed."

Renee just wanted the best for Scott, no matter what, but secretly she was relieved that Kessler prevailed over Mt. Sinai. Scott had never been to New York City in his life. West Orange, New Jersey, where Kessler is located, is a congested suburb less than an hour from Manhattan, but it seemed the much safer option. "None of us are used to the city," Renee says laughing. "Kessler may not be the country, but it's not New York either. Can you imagine it? That would have been like the Beverly Hillbillies in New York. Totally wouldn't work."

Scott's accident may have been the most unlucky, most unfair thing in the world, but in everything that had happened to her boy since that moment, Gert was convinced that there was more than luck at work. "They say the Lord works in marvelous ways, and I do believe that. Nobody can tell me there's no such a thing as angels. I mean I know the Lord sends his angels, but I tell you there were angels watching over Scott. I truly believe that. I just know there was."

And one of them actually came down to earth. It must have been divine intervention, because things looked a lot brighter for Scott when Toni Longshore entered the picture. Toni was the independent caseworker assigned to Scott by his insurance company to, as she puts it, "assist with the coordination of medical treatment." That cut-and-dried job description, however, doesn't come close to capturing the role that Toni would play in his life from the immediate aftermath of the accident to his transfer to Kessler and way, way beyond. She worked with Scott's doctors, the discharge nurses, and the social workers at the hospital to prepare for Scott's transfer to Kessler. Throughout his rehab, his transition home, and his ongoing care, she monitored Scott's status regularly, speaking to him, his family, nurses, doctors, and therapists. She would be Scott's voice to the insurance company in every single move, including getting the right people to look over Scott's home, getting construction quotes, making sure that his home was remodeled for accessibility, and coordinating his therapy and doctors' visits after he came home.

She also became a friend. She regularly called to ask Scott how things were going, and he came to find comfort in unloading on her. She took it for granted that that was all part of answering his needs. "When you have such a traumatic injury, there's a point where you don't believe it, and all of a sudden it hits you, and you get really depressed," she says. "I've seen Scott really depressed. You have those days when you just kind of lose it, and it's good to have somebody to talk to. So a lot of my clients, like Scott, will just call and then they'll feel better, and that's what I'm there for."

That's not exactly the stereotype that most people have of the relatively anonymous agents who tend to be connected to their insurance companies. In fact, Toni says she knows other people who serve as freelance case managers like she does, and, for a lot of them, their work is "strictly business."

"I guess it's my background," she figures. "I worked in rehab and different aspects of human services for so long before I got into this field, and it's part of my nature. I'm hired by the insurance company, but my job is to advocate for the injured person." Toni's brand of advocacy meant getting Scott the services and care he needed, and recognizing that "when people have injuries, especially like Scott's, they just don't know what to do, they don't know how to deal with it."

So Toni became instrumental in helping to activate the first major decision that Scott would make for his after-life, his transfer to Kessler Institute.

At the same time, the Remingtons were making another profound decision. Gert, Bull, Denise, Earle, Steph, and Renee resolved that none of the Remington men would log ever again.

It is ironic that, at the time of his accident, Scott had been making plans to broaden his business interests in ways that would gradually shift him out of active logging. But it was excruciating to think that a change this big was now being driven by circumstances beyond his control. He was being forced out of the woods by accident.

8.

A man *of* the woods

As he neared his high school graduation in 1984, Scott toyed with the idea of joining the navy. He had seen the naval bases where Denise and Kevin had been stationed, and Kevin had taken Scott to work with him a couple of times at Pearl Harbor when Scott had visited them in Hawaii. Around that time, one of Scott's classmates, as well as his cousin, Jimmy, were planning to go into the air force, and the whole idea of military service had an adventurous appeal. But a hernia operation sidelined Scott long enough to change his mind.

After graduation, he got a place with his buddy, Chris Johnson, who had graduated the year before, and Scott decided to start his working life in the comfort zone, in the woods with his dad and Uncle Jim at Remington Brothers.

Scott worked as a professional lumberman for nearly three years until 1987, when a new power line was slated to go through the area, and Asplundh Tree Expert

Company, a large utility industry contractor, came in to clear the vegetation and create the access roads for the new line. Scott's cousin, Benny, was working for Asplundh and asked Scott if he wanted to come aboard. Scott jumped. "We'd be cutting trees, and I'd be learning how to climb—real high, maybe fifty to seventy feet up. I'd also be running the heavy equipment, like the bulldozers, and I wanted to get into that more, so I said, 'Sure.'" Chris, who had gone back and forth between excavating and logging, jumped ship about a year after Scott and went to work for Asplundh, too, along with another of Scott's high school friends, Jim Peck.

Life was just right—earning good money, running big machines, playing hard, and living with Chris. "*That* was a good experience," says Scott about the two apartments that he and Chris shared. "Oh boy, that was something else. A lot of fun. Good times."

When the power line was complete, Asplundh offered the guys a chance to travel, and they took that, too. One of their first assignments was around Watertown, way up in the northwest corner of New York State near the Ontario border, where they cleaned up after a series of ice storms. Then life really got interesting.

On October 6, 1989, twenty-three-year-old Scott married twenty-year-old Cindy Eastman. They had known each other in high school, Scott had even kissed her in the hall a few times, but they hadn't started dating seriously until after Scott graduated. Their first baby, John, whom the family nicknamed "Roscoe," came along in 1991, just when Scott really started spending serious time on the road. He went down to Maryland and worked most of one summer, and then, when Cindy was pregnant with their daughter, Jenna, Scott was assigned to a site in South Carolina near Savannah. The job lasted from June to September of 1992. Scott would fly home every couple of weeks, but it was clear that the work/life balance was coming unhinged.

Everything about the job was near perfect. "I was making good money for my family, no question about that," says Scott. "All the guys I worked with were great, and I was doing what I liked, running all kinds of equipment." The crew was clearing woods and making roads for new transmission lines and "killing at least one or two poisonous snakes a day down there."

Things at home were less than perfect. Living the life of a single parent was not what Cindy had in mind, and it tore her apart every time Scott had to get on the plane to go back to work. Fortunately, when the job ended down south, Asplundh gave Scott an assignment closer to home. He was put on a project in Plattsburgh, New York that winter, which had him commuting about an hour each way. At least he was home every night, but there was still precious little family time. He was trying to figure out his next move, when his uncle Jim came to him and said, "Your dad and I are giving up the logging business, do you want it?"

At the age of twenty-eight, Scott became the owner of the family business, paying his dad and uncle every month for most of the next five years until he covered the $50,000 purchase price. Jim started a new excavating business, and Scott asked his dad and brother to stay on and work for him. Over the roughly six years that Scott ran the business, he also hired several different men to drive the pulp truck. He was no longer in command of Asplundh's massive earthmovers, and he gave up the chance to travel, but Scott had stumbled onto a new source of challenge, excitement, and, ultimately, pressure. Being his own boss and making Remington Logging more than a good business—making it a success—became his passion.

He is quick to credit his dad and uncle with helping him financially in the early years. He insists that he never would have been as successful without their support. But he drove the company with a young man's energy and ambition, and, although that sometimes created friction between Scott and his dad, the rewards quickly became evident. Scott invested aggressively in new equipment. The pulp truck, for instance, set him back $65,000 for the cab and chassis and another $15,000 for the trailer, and a used loader went for about $60,000. He also expanded his roster of contracts. Bull had had long-standing relationships with a short list of mills and was concerned that his son might be moving too far too fast. But even he couldn't argue with the results, and it was clear to everyone who worked with Scott that he was not only a clever businessman but also scrupulously honest.

Marty Mead ran the truck for Scott for four or five years. In his sixties, Marty had been in the business a long time, and he knew that, "It's hard for a young person to tell an older person what to do, but I always got along great with Scott." No matter who Marty worked for, he refused to "drive illegal," hauling any load that exceeded the weight limit specified on a company's truck permit. That was never an issue with Scott. "I didn't want to run a truck unless it was running legal," says Marty. "Some guys don't care and just take their chances, but I won't." Scott had a permit to haul up to 102,000 pounds, and he was firm about staying within that upper limit. Most Remington loads, says Marty, weighed in around 92,000 pounds.

Marty had also known lots of loggers who bought heavier, more powerful trucks so they could travel faster, but that meant that they couldn't carry as much wood, because so much of the weight limit was taken up by the truck itself. "Scott could carry more wood," he says, "because he bought a lighter truck without as much power." Marty admired that decision from a business perspective, just like he admired the work ethic of his young boss.

"He's a worker," Marty says of Scott. "The work is hard work, and it's a hard business to be in. You got to be disciplined, because you got to go to work whether you feel like it or not. When you're in business for yourself, you can't say 'I'll sleep a little longer this morning.' You got to work with the weather. You can't rule Mother Nature, you work regardless. Too many of them nowadays don't, and that's why they just can't make it. But he loved it. You gotta love it to be in this business. If you don't, there's no sense to try it, because you just can't make it. Scott would have made it if he hadn't been hurt, I'm sure of it."

Along with the considerable work he was doing for Finch, Pruyn and some other area mills, Scott was forging relationships with foresters who were increasingly recommending him to their private landowner-clients.

Brent Bullock, a forester and log buyer who has a log yard in Chestertown, was one. He hired Scott and his crew to cut marked timber on a couple of privately owned lots. Brent explains that, as the consulting forester on jobs like these, he would go in and mark the trees to be cut, hire the logger to do the cutting, and negotiate with the logger on a price for the wood. Then the logger would sell the timber to a mill or lumberyard and share the revenue, based on their contract, with the forester and landowner.

Scott "was young and really just getting started," Brent recalls, "but he ran a real good business. He just likes the woods—just likes being around trees—and he was modernizing as much as he could. The equipment he got from his father and his uncle were older machines. He bought a new truck, a new loader, and I think a couple of skidders, too. He was constantly upgrading, and I think if he had been able to stay in business, he certainly would have been one of the better loggers available now."

It was more than shiny, new machines that made Brent recommend Scott to his clients. When Brent hires someone, the amount of supervision they require is one of his primary concerns. As the liaison between the logger and the landowner, he's always concerned that the logger is only cutting the marked wood, isn't causing too much damage to the residual stand, and is processing the trees in a way that will get the most value out of them. "That's what I look for," says Brent, "and Scott did a good job that way. I didn't have to be there all the time to look after them and make sure that things were done good and done right."

Jim Farrar is another consulting forester who sent major work to Scott over about a three- or four-year period. Jim represents landowners, advising them about how to manage their timberlands for optimal growth, and, like Brent, he represents the owners when it comes to the sale of the timber. In 1994, Jim had a client who needed to complete a timber sale that had already been started. After inspecting the woodlot with Jim, Scott accepted the job, launching a relationship that both Jim and Scott remember with fondness and respect.

For Jim, Scott scored on all fronts. Besides having the requisite equipment and insurance, Jim was looking for "the quality of the wood work." "Logging is an inherently destructive type of business with big machines cutting big trees," he explains. "I'm trying to control the harvest so the property grows quality timber in the future." So, Jim constantly watches to be sure that the loggers he hires get the trees cut and out of the woods to the landing area with a minimal amount of damage to unmarked trees. "Some loggers are just better at controlling the damage than others," he says, "because of their personalities and their willingness to put the effort into doing a quality job in the woods." Scott was one of them.

Scott never disappointed on the payments end either. "The other thing I'm looking for is, do they pay regularly?" says Jim. "Do I have to routinely chase them for payments to my landowners? With Scott, there was never a problem."

Making those payments was as much a function of honesty as business savvy. In negotiating a price with a forester, Scott had to secure a buyer for the wood, know how much that buyer, whether it was a mill or lumberyard, would pay, and have the skill to process the wood in a way that would maximize the dollars he could get. That's a complicated calculus.

For the logger, Jim explains, "equipment is expensive, breakdowns are expensive, and then there's the weather conditions. If you've got a lot of rainy weather and the woods get muddy, production slows down. You've also got rugged terrain, steep slopes, rocky terrain— all these are factors that limit how you can maneuver equipment through the woods. You've got to recognize all this in managing your cash flow. You've got obligations in payments to your men, payments for withholding for taxes, and you've got to control all this."

Market conditions, too, can derail a lot of timber jobs. Some loggers stop in the middle of a cut and move on to other jobs, because the particular species they're cutting suddenly becomes less salable. Whether it's due to a revised cost-benefit analysis or simply an undependable cutter, unfinished work makes life tough on the forester. "It just makes it more difficult to keep track of records and what happened and where you're supposed to pick up after a few months. Things get missed in the woods," says Jim. "But whenever Scott took on a job for me, he'd say, 'Here's what I'm doing now, here's about when I'll be available.' Once he moved to the job, he'd complete it, whether it was a month or three months work, he stayed from start to finish."

And Scott wasn't prone to tantrums. With some loggers, Jim would brace himself as soon as the jobs began. "You'd just expect as soon as you get into an arrangement with them, there's going to be some whining, or they didn't think of this or that, or this is going to cost me more money than I anticipated. That didn't occur with Scott. He and his father and his brother worked together, and things just moved along in an orderly, businesslike way. If there was a problem of any kind, we discussed it. It didn't get to be a big thing. Whatever it was, we solved it and continued working."

Owning up to problems, whatever they were, came in particularly handy the day Scott accidentally met Nick deGregory, who had a vacation place on Brant Lake. Nick and his wife owned acreage both on the lake and across the road. One weekend, they drove up to their place and noticed that someone had cut a logging trail through their woods. Nick and his wife went up to inspect it and discovered that whoever had been cutting on the adjacent land had made a turn that cut across their property. It was unfortunate, but, to be honest, says Nick, "it was not a big thing to my wife or myself," so they didn't think any more about it and spent a peaceful weekend on the lake.

That Monday evening, though, back at their home in Queensbury, New York, the phone rang. "Hello Mr. deGregory, my name is Scott Remington," said the young man on the phone. "I just bought my logging business from my uncle and dad, and my father's cousin tells me that I cut across your property on the corner." Nick answered, "Yeah, it appears that way, but I'll tell you what, I'll be up next Sunday, why don't you meet me up there, and we'll take a look at it and discuss it." Scott said that would be fine.

Nick hadn't hung up the phone two minutes, when it rang again. It was his cousin's son, Jay, who was about Scott's age. For the hell of it, Nick asked him, "Hey Jay, do you know a fellow by the name of Scott Remington?" Nick remembers that he "actually could hear the smile in Jay's voice."

Jay told him, "Scott! What a great guy! We went to school together, I know his parents, I dated his sister, Renee. What's going on?" Nick told him about the call from Scott, and Jay was all over it, telling Nick, "Cut him some slack! He's the greatest."

Scott met Nick that next Sunday, and Nick recalls, "My first impression of Scott was his smile. He had such a genuine smile, and I could see why Jay and he gravitated together. They're two people you just couldn't not like. It's something, I don't know how else to put it." Nick established that Scott was fully insured, but of course, in this situation, what's done is done. This was really simply an opportunity for Scott to meet Nick face-to-face and say he was sorry. So Nick just asked Scott to keep the woods neat while he was working up in there—Nick didn't want to find empty oil jugs and oil filters lying in the woods. "His honesty went a long way," says Nick. "He was so genuine. And he finished up his logging there and kept to his word."

In fact, Nick thought so much of Scott that he hired Scott about a year later to thin the timber on his land, and the two men have been friends ever since. Nick remembers when he first heard about Scott's accident. "My first feeling was, gee, God can't take that smile out of the world. It's too important." To this day, Nick is amazed at how "it was really a thing that stunned the whole community. Such a hardworking guy, gorgeous family, I never heard anyone say a negative word about him, and it was just so unfair. But as someone once told me, the Lord never gives you more weight than your shoulders can bear. And I'll tell you, he's bearing up real good."

Nick and his wife have since retired to the lake, and rather than just kicking back and taking it easy, Nick was talked into resuming an old avocation by a friend who was working up at Jimbo's. He took up bartending at the restaurant, and Scott, before and after his accident, would stop by to say hi and have a couple of drinks. And more than once, Scott has been blindsided by the "Nickarita"—Nick's killer margarita. Few feats require more determination than negotiating a wheelchair after a couple of those.

In just his first couple of years as a business owner, Scott managed both to capitalize on and strengthen the Remington name, which set him up for a particularly important opportunity when nature unleashed its vengeance in July of 1995.

It was an exceptionally hot month. Sweltering temperatures lasted unabated for a couple of weeks. Then, at 6:00 in the morning on July 15, a massive front change brewed a series of severe thunderstorms and sent straight-line winds whipping through the Adirondacks.

Straight-line winds are easily confused with tornadoes, because of their speed—blowing upwards of one hundred miles an hour—and their destructive power. Unlike swirling tornadoes, though, these winds blow horizontally, which is why their telltale damage pattern often includes uprooted trees laying practically in parallel rows. On that particular day in the Adirondacks, the National Weather Service reported that, in some counties, mobile homes and other structures were tossed hundreds of feet, debris was scattered over a half-mile swath, roofs were torn off many permanent structures, power was knocked out for days, and thousands of trees were felled.

This was precisely the scene that met Tom McPhillips when he inspected one of his family's timber lots on Collins Mountain just south of North Creek, New York. Tom's family has lived in the area since the 1850s, and that lot had been in the family for more than a hundred years. "This was a beautiful timber lot with a lot of nice maple and good quality pine," says Tom, "but the hand of God doesn't pick and choose. Out of this hundred-and-fifty-acre lot, about a hundred acres were completely flat. It looked like matchsticks."

Tom got in touch with his forester, Jim Farrar, and told him, "I gotta get somebody in there who's not gonna muck it up." Jim said that Scott Remington was the man. Jim spoke highly of Scott, but given the massive job and the potential value of the fallen wood, Tom did some independent research. He talked to other landowners and learned that "Scott had taken every logger training and safety course you could imagine. I knew that he was a very good, very competent logger. And I knew he was honest as the driven snow."

Unfortunately, says Tom, honesty is at a premium in the logging and timber business. "There's what you call cut-and-runners—people who will cut and they'll run, and you don't even know they've been on your land." There are also guys who might process ten trailer-loads of logs, but pay the landowner for nine, and "you don't know it, but Scott, never. Always right up front. Scott is a north-country, backwoods, honest-as-the-driven-snow, what-you-see-is-what-you-get kinda guy."

Tom and Scott went up to the property to survey the damage, and, while they were there, Tom asked Scott to thin another fifty-acre adjoining parcel. "It made sense as long as he was going to be up there," says Tom. "This was back in the woods, about a mile off any town road. Once you're in there with the equipment, and you're all set up to go, you might as well do it."

Starting in the fall of 1995, it took Scott, Bull, Earle, and a couple of guys Scott had hired, nearly a year to complete the job. They did such a good job under very difficult circumstances that Tom immediately thought of Scott when another dicey situation came up.

Tom needed to clear-cut a ten-acre parcel that his family was selling to the small town of Thurman, New York. The parcel sat next to the Thurman landfill, and the town needed the parcel's sandy soil to cover the landfill. Since the family was selling the land only, they wanted to harvest all the timber off the lot before they turned it over to the town, a job that took Scott and company another year. "This lot was in the middle of a two-hundred-and-fifty-acre timber lot, which was up and down mountains and very, very tough," says Tom. "Scott did an absolutely tremendous job over there."

Tom was sold. He decided right then that he'd have Scott working on and off for his family for the next thirty years. It broke his heart when their professional relationship ended in less than three. Their friendship, though, endures. Says Tom, "Scott has a personality, when he smiles you can just look at him and see that it's as genuine as possible. I think I'm a pretty good judge of folks, and I knew when I first met him that what you see is what you get. I'm glad that I'm able to call him a friend."

Scott's glad, too. "I wish I was still working for Tom. Jim [Farrar] was marking for him—we were a great team. Jim would come and sit down and have lunch with us in the woods, and my dad and Earle and I would tell him all our hunting stories, and we had a great time. And Tom and his wife, Lois, became friends with me and Cindy, and we had lots of good times. Sometimes you don't mix business with pleasure, but Tom and Lois and me and Cindy had a lot of fun. Tom likes his beer—loves those microbrews—and I like a few beers, and we loved to talk."

Tell Scott how people size him up as a friend and a professional, and he is deeply flattered and a little surprised. To do a job right, to pay his clients what he promised, was intuitive. It would be like getting a pat on the back for his straight blond hair and strong, square build.

"You take your time to try to make a nice job is what I did. You'd look at the situation and figure out the best way to get the trees out without damaging the most timber. If you had six trees to hitch, you look and figure out what's the best way to cut those six trees without tearing down the whole timber. And if you got a real big pine tree, and you know it's gonna knock something down, you fell it where it's gonna knock the least amount down. But if you do knock something else down, you might as well pick it up and scrape up the area. The tree's gonna die anyway.

"But Jim Farrar is being generous when he says it was all my skill. Jim made my job easy, too, because he was so good at marking. A lot of foresters will mark a tree up and just expect you to get it out. Jim was great at selecting trees that were in good position.

"But look, if you do a good, clean job, they give you more work. If you rip somebody off, it gets around. It's just a matter of time. A lot of people take that risk, but I can't see taking something dishonest. I'd rather tell somebody I can't pay as much for their wood, but the upside is I'll pay them for the whole thing, instead of promising them a lot of money and not paying them for half of what I take. A lot of landowners will tell you, 'Hey this other logger is gonna pay me a lot more for my wood.' I tell them, 'Yeah, but he's not gonna pay you for all of it.'"

Between 1993 and 1999, when Scott ran Remington Logging, he was in his element. "I was successful," he says with no boast in his voice. "I was making good money. There's a lot of hassles of running your own business, and it was stressful, but I enjoyed it. I was comfortable in it." He was, however, also recognizing that the long hours and dangers of the business were not the best things for himself or his young family. So when his uncle offered to teach him the excavating business, he saw opportunity. He could hire some men to help him keep the logging business going, while he built up an excavating operation at the same time. It was a perfect plan. "I was going to expand, and have both things going at once, and I wouldn't be doing such dangerous work every day," he says. "It was all set. My uncle was going to teach me the ropes. Then I… then I got hurt."

Scott was certainly open to change. He was willing to reinvent himself. In fact, in spite of how much he loved the logging business, he was getting excited to start a new chapter, because it was part of a plan, and it was on his terms.

In May of 1999, the terms of his life became unrecognizable to him and to Cindy.

The earth was turned on its head. Everything big, like work and family routines and camping trips, was pushed off the front burner. Everything little, like how you're going to get into the shower and onto the toilet and in and out of the car, became all-consuming. And when you're hit with that new reality, you honestly can't sort out which is the most profound loss, the big things or the little things.

Like scores of people throughout the community, Renee's friend, Ellen McDermott, who owned the flower shop in Chestertown, followed Scott's tragedy from afar. But Ellen followed it with a special understanding. Ellen had lost her brother when he was nineteen years old, and she couldn't help comparing the sense of loss inherent in both situations. Whether it's a death or a life-altering event, "you're really losing that person," she says. When she lost her brother, she had to come to grips with the fact that "that person is really and truly gone as you knew him." And that same thought haunted her when she thought about Scott. "He's not going to ever be the same person again. So you grieve for that, and I'm sure Scott grieves for that. He had to make himself a new person."

You will be hard-pressed to find a more succinct summary of the recovery experience—a grueling emotional and physical process of reinventing yourself by mastering a thousand new routines, learning to live inside a strange body, getting used to a new reflection in the mirror. But enduring that process is the only way to right the world, so that the little stuff and the big stuff can, to whatever extent possible, reclaim their rightful places.

Part II

I was never sick a day in my life and then, boom!, it hits you. Same with Scott, I mean there's a danger level to what he did, but he goes out and does what he's been doing for years, and all of a sudden... The biggest thing is you just gotta keep hoping and keep pushing, because hopefully one of these days, they'll come up with an answer for this.

Joe Rizzi, one of Scott's roommates at Kessler, who became an "incomplete quad" at the age of fifty when a freak staph infection caused an abscess that squeezed his spine at the C5 level.

*****

The mindset of the handicapped person is amazing. I would love to know how [Scott] thinks, because of the way he was cut down in life so quick, the prime of his life... Once you've been there and seen what they've gone through, the treatments they've gone through, and what's been done to their bodies. There's no hold-back anymore for them. I mean, they've been stripped, done over, remade... and yes in the beginning they were very angry, very hurt, but now... The last time I saw [Scott], he's not holding back anything. Buddy's the same way. He figures, 'Hey, you don't like the way I look? Don't look at me!

Barbara Mullaney, whose son Buddy was another of Scott's Kessler roommates. Buddy was eighteen and waiting to receive his orders to join an elite unit of the air force when he was paralyzed in a car accident.

9.

You can't make this up

It was like an omen foreshadowing the long, strange trip that Scott was about to experience in New Jersey and beyond. Or maybe it was just one of life's sick jokes. But the trip from Burlington, Vermont to the Kessler Institute in New Jersey simply defied imagination.

Scott was discharged from Fletcher Allen around 8:00 in the morning on June 11, 1999 and put on a small propeller plane for the flight to New Jersey. Cindy and Renee left Burlington as soon as they knew that Scott was in the ambulance and on his way to the airport. With a five-hour drive ahead of them, they wanted to get going and figured they'd meet up with Scott after he was safely checked in at Kessler.

Scott took off on time. Mid-flight, though, the pilot sensed trouble. He radioed to Schenectady County Airport in Scotia, New York, and made an emergency landing. Engine trouble. An ambulance was called to the airport, and Scott was unloaded into the vehicle, which sat on the runway for four hours until another plane could arrive from Buffalo. It was a beastly day, and Scott was immobilized on a stretcher in his neck brace and plastic body jacket. "Had to be the high nineties," he says, "and, oh man, sitting in that ambulance. I still remember that nurse asking me if I wanted a milkshake. I said, 'God no! I just want to *go* somewhere.'"

He was finally loaded onto another plane that took him to an airport in Fairfield, New Jersey, where he was transferred to another ambulance for the ride to Kessler, except that the driver headed off to Kessler's rehab facility in *East* Orange, "the one that does a lot of brain stuff," says Scott. He didn't reach the right Kessler in West Orange until around 8:00 that evening, capping off a twelve-hour odyssey.

Meanwhile, Cindy and Renee found their way to Kessler and asked to see Scott Remington. They were told that he hadn't arrived. "We were in a panic," says Renee. "So they allowed us to use the phone to call back to Burlington, and they have no idea where Scott is." After asking around, the Burlington staff informed Renee that there had been a problem with the plane. "By the time Scott got there—twelve hours later!" she says, "he was so wiped out. But it was just one more thing in those first three months—y'know, what else can go wrong?"

Also waiting and worrying was Dr. Barbara Benevento, Kessler's clinical chief of spinal cord injury services, who would oversee Scott's care. Most patients making the transition from the hospital to rehab arrive feeling overwhelmed. Dr. Benevento sees it all the time, the trauma of their conditions combined with the switch to a new place is enormously disorienting. Scott was especially overwrought. "By the time he got here, he was just spent," she says. "He was very quiet. We did most of the talking."

After everything that Scott had been through, his day was not quite over. He still had to undergo the standard intake assessment for all new patients. Although Dr. Benevento and her team have pored over the hospital records of their new patients prior to their arrival, they do their own thorough examinations and take their own histories as soon as they meet their patients. "We want to know what the patient knows and what they remember," she explains, and they run patients through an ASIA exam, the standardized physical assessment developed by the American Spinal Injury Association.

The exam gives doctors and therapists anywhere in the country a standard tool and a standard language with which to characterize the extent of a spinal cord injury. As doctors follow patients over time, the test also gives them a point of reference to determine levels of progress.

The ASIA exam has three parts. The first is a function test. Dr. Benevento asked Scott to move different parts of his body—arms, wrists, elbow flexors, abductors, trunk muscles, hip flexors, knee extensors, dorsal flexors—both with and against gravity, and she filled in scores on the outline of a human body depicted on a data sheet. She was looking to see if there was some movement or no movement at all, and, if there was no movement, whether she could at least feel muscles working. On a scale of zero to five, where zero is no movement and five is full movement, "what we're hoping to get are muscles that are three or better," she says, "because those are the muscles that you can do a lot with." Scott's chart shows a stark division—fives all the way down the cervical region into the mid-back area, then zeroes from the mid-thoracic area down through the lumbar and sacral regions.

After that, there were two sensation exams. Dr. Benevento touched Scott all over his body, first using a cotton swab to test "light touch," then using a safety pin. For both tests, she began by touching Scott's face with the swab and then the blunt end of the pin. The sensation he felt on his face would serve as his point of reference. As she made her way down his body, she asked him, "Does it feel like your face, not like your face, or you don't feel it at all." Anything that felt like his face scored a two. If he didn't feel it at all, he got a zero. If he felt something, but it wasn't exactly like his face, he got a one. If he felt something with the dull side of the pin, but it wasn't like his face, she had him try to distinguish between the sharp side and the dull side of the pin.

For both touch tests, Scott scored perfectly all the way down to T9, then at T10 he had "a little impaired sensation," followed by zeroes. Dr. Benevento was able to conclude that, in the language of the spinal cord injured or SCI community, "he was a T9." That is, his ninth thoracic vertebra, just above the belly button, was his sensory cutoff point.

It was important for Dr. Benevento to determine his "level," not only so that she knew what she was dealing with, but also, she points out, "because it gives us an idea of prognosis." With therapy, someone with a complete injury can usually regain one level of sensation. In Scott's case, her expectation was that he would recover some feeling and control at T10, the belly button range. "When you're in that thoracic region," she explains, "people may think, *Big deal, so I gained a little bit back, I still can't move my legs.*" But gaining that level back, just the distance from one vertebra to another, can mean a lot when it comes to balance and the ability to transfer your body from one place to another. "Everything's a big deal when you don't have a lot of strength. What you gain back is a big deal, even if it's just sensation. It gives you a little better idea of where things are. Even in the thoracic region, it's important."

In fact, she was exactly correct. Months later, after Scott left Kessler and began therapy back home at Glens Falls Hospital, his patient records show him with a diagnosis of T10.

Beyond testing movement and feeling, one of the most critical goals of the intake assessment is to determine what doctors call "sacral sparing." At the very end of the spine, below the low back or lumbar vertebrae, there are five smaller vertebrae that are fused together into one solid piece, known as the sacrum. The sacrum leads to the bottom tip of the spine—the coccyx or tailbone. Being close to the rectum, nerves in the sacral segments control signals and sensation in the groin and parts of the legs. Thus, sacral sparing refers to how much, if any, rectal sensation and function is spared after an injury. Dr. Benevento touched both the swab and pin to Scott's rectum; he felt neither. She inserted her finger into his rectum and asked him if he could feel it, then she asked him to squeeze down to see if he had any ability to contract those muscles. He could not.

So, here he was—in New Jersey, now, fourteen to fifteen hours post-Vermont, with his nerve endings ablaze, after two planes and three ambulances, and he's had to process responses to: We're experiencing engine trouble. How about a milkshake? Hang in there buddy, wrong hospital. Can you feel my finger in your rectum?

It had been some enchanted evening.

Perhaps the only bright spot in the whole surreal adventure was that, if he had to get that intimate with someone on the first date, at least it was with Barbara Benevento. She is a professional with impeccable credentials. Besides overseeing patient rehabilitation at Kessler, she is on the faculty at the University of Medicine and Dentistry of New Jersey, where her students once named her "Teacher of the Year." Her specialties include amputee rehab, musculoskeletal and neurological disorders, and pain management, and she directs Kessler's Neurocontrol Freehand System Clinic.

She is also warm, outgoing, and instantly able to make a stranger feel like a friend. Unless she is tied up in a meeting or with a patient, she is striding through the halls at Kessler, in and out of the clinics, gyms, and swimming pool room, checking up on her patients and staff, high-fiving, laying on a comforting hand, joking around, remembering to ask patients how things are going at home, or lifting a hand that has fallen off the armrest of a wheelchair and gently putting it back in place. She knows an astounding number of first names, and, as she makes her rounds, people constantly call out to her to get her attention. She cries with her patients over their triumphs and setbacks, lets out whoops of joy over their good news, goes to the mat with their insurers, prods patients to do one more rep in the gym, lets them wallow if they need to, and knows when to order them to get off their butts and work harder.

She is a skilled physician and researcher, who's intensely attuned to the profound emotional dimension of her patients' conditions. About the ASIA exam, she is quick to point out that, "It all sounds very nice on paper, but if you're the patient trying to figure out—Do I feel that? Do I not feel that? What are they talking about?—while people are walking in and out of the room, and bells are going off in the building—it's tough. With some patients, the exam takes hours."

She understands that, in particular, the exam for sacral sparing—like the regimens that must soon be mastered to deal with bowel and bladder function—is an initiation rite that tests the depths of her patients' characters. Everyone handles that exam differently, she explains. "They come with their own baggage—their histories of how they were raised, how they deal with things emotionally, do they cry, do they not cry, do they talk? A lot of men tend to be more closed, women tend to talk more. But there's no person who will ever be the same."

In Dr. Benevento's company, it's surprising how quickly you get used to discussing all things excretory. Within moments, it's not so uncomfortable to say words like stool, urine, bowel, bladder, and sphincter out loud. These words are the nuts and bolts of her trade. A huge part of her job is to reintroduce her patients to subjects that they haven't thought about consciously since the age of about three or four. For her spinal cord injured patients, these are things that take on entirely new significance in daily life.

The process of relearning how to go to the bathroom is one that Dr. Lauren Vocaturo, Kessler's clinical manager of the Department of Psychology and Neuropsychology, calls "the harsh destruction of dignity that patients have to deal with."

It involves learning how to self-catheterize in order to urinate, which at this point in Scott's life, meant inserting a tube into his penis every four to six hours to empty his bladder. It involves mastering what's called the "bowel program," that is, inserting a suppository into the rectum every day to relax the sphincter and loosen the stool, then using a finger or plastic device to help the stool vacate the rectum, a process called "digital stimulation." The days of "holding it" until it's convenient to go, and then dashing in and out of the bathroom, are over.

In the spinal cord injured body, the bowel—the part of the intestine that's below the stomach—continues to operate like nothing's wrong, feeding waste material down to the rectum. The patient, however, can no longer control the release of waste because of the disconnect between the brain and spine. "You can go all the time," Dr. Benevento explains. "You're always incontinent." So she told Scott, as she does all her patients, "We have to trick the bowel to do what we want it to do." It's all about timing and getting your body into a defecation rhythm.

On his first full day at the center, Scott received medication to clean out the lower section of the bowel. Then, the following morning, when the stool at the top of the bowel had moved down, he was ready to learn his program—to learn how to clean himself out for the day. And that's how it would be every day. Get up in the morning, insert a suppository, wait for it to work, then help the stool out. In other words, a big part of the afterlife is accepting that having a bowel movement is a process that can easily take an hour out of every day.

"I have a patient who went back to work on Wall Street following a spinal cord injury," Dr. Benevento explains. "He gets up at 4:30 every morning to do his bowel regimen and then goes off for the day. I'm ashamed of myself for complaining that I get up at six."

All of this is assuming that a whole host of complications don't gum up the works, and "what happens to the bowel happens to the bladder and vice versa," says Dr. Benevento. "They all live in the same area." When you're using a catheter to urinate, it's frustratingly easy to contract urinary tract infections, given that a tube must be regularly inserted into the bladder. What's more, any number of medications that an SCI patient may take, including antibiotics, can dry the stool, which can throw off the bowel program by trapping stool in the bowel and potentially introducing bacteria into the bladder, which can lead to infection.

Similarly, spasticity, a common complication of spinal cord injury, sends muscles—including the bladder—into involuntary spasms, which can cause leaking. Medication to stop the bladder from squeezing can also dry the stool, causing constipation that wreaks havoc with bowel rhythm. It can be a nasty cycle, and the threats of accidents and infections never go away.

Of course, at this point, Scott could only *understand* his program, he couldn't do it himself. He was learning about his regimen as he was healing from surgery and bound into a body jacket, so it was physically impossible to lean over and self-cath or reach his rectum on his own. As a result, he faced a special brand of humiliation known to many of his SCI brothers and sisters. The nurses had to do these things for him, and the nurses had to teach his wife and sister to do them as well.

"I learned his bowel program and the cath routine," says Renee. "That's a hard thing to do with your sister. Cindy learned, too, and we'd take turns, because she'd get exhausted, and because, what happens if one of us gets sick? You have to have backup." Then she pauses, and you can hear the shift, the softening in her tone that tells you she's trying to picture in her mind what life looks like through her brother's eyes. "I remember him saying, 'Oh God, you're my sister.' And I'd say, 'Yeah, but I'm also a nurse. Don't worry about it.' To have to give someone a suppository… that was hard for him, but for some reason he let me do it. Because of that, there will always be a closeness between us. Think of what he's allowed me to be a part of. I am just so grateful that… Gosh… I'm sorry, it makes me teary… that I had the chance to be that major person for him."

Dr. Vocaturo regularly jokes with her post-doctoral interns that, "We went through a hundred years of higher education to talk about bowel and bladder and sexual function all day." But it is hardly surprising that those issues dominate so many discussions with patients. They represent the ultimate loss of privacy. It is why Dr. Benevento hears time after time, "I'd rather never walk again if I could just have my bladder and bowel function back."

Showering was another strange, new ordeal. Patients are on a schedule; Scott's days were Tuesdays and Thursdays. "I was used to showering every day, so I couldn't wait to be washed," he says. "I felt really grungy when my day rolled around." Harold, a Kessler staff member, who Scott remembers as a "big, tall, African-American guy, had to be over six feet," would get Scott undressed in his room, cover him with a blanket, and wheel him down the hall and into the shower room. The undressing process involved rolling Scott from one side to the other to get his clothes off and transferring him to a shower-stretcher—both of which made him see stars. It also involved changing Scott's cervical collar to one that he could be showered in. "I couldn't sit up without the plastic shell, so that's why they had to wash me on a stretcher, a special one that the water can go through, and I had to have the neck thing on the whole time. Harold just unhooked it to wash there, then hooked it back up."

It was embarrassing, especially at first, because Harold had to wash Scott everywhere. "He'd scrub my arms and body, and lift up my legs to make sure I was clean, but he really tried to make me feel comfortable. I remember he liked to fish and we talked about that." After a while, though, Scott talked Cindy into taking over the washing job. "I asked her to please do it. Harold was a great guy, but he was kinda rough. It wasn't his fault, but I was just so sensitive from all the rib injuries. It just hurt so much, so they let her do it. We figured we had to get ready to go home anyway."

Excretion and showering were only the beginning. Kessler doesn't waste a moment of its patients' precious time. Classes begin immediately.

Renee wheeled Scott to his first class, because Cindy had gone back home to help the children finish up the school year. The subject was decubitus ulcers. Decubitus, from the Latin verb *decumbere*—to lie down—is a synonym for bedsore, and such sores are constant threats to people who sit or lie on their backs or sides for long periods of time without moving.

Like a stealth bomb, the ulcer develops, and a person usually has no idea that it's happening until it's too late. They are pressure sores that begin forming deep within the body where a bone presses against internal tissue. That constant, unrelenting pressure causes an irritation that increases in intensity over time moving outward through more and more layers of tissue until it reaches the skin. By the time a decubitus is evident, because of redness on the skin or an actual hole that has broken through the skin, it's too late for preventive treatment. The sore extends all the way down to the bone. It's therefore imperative that paralyzed patients make a habit of shifting their weight constantly throughout the day. If they are unable to shift on their own, their caregivers must be diligent about doing it for them.

"We see these slides," Renee recalls. "They show this person's bottom with a hole—a huge, open ulcer—that you could put somebody's fist into, and they say this is what will happen if you don't do weight shift." Scott couldn't take it. He broke down and told his sister, "Get me out of here!" She wheeled him back to his room, and they sobbed together as he repeated, "I can't do this. I can't do this."

Through her own tears, Renee told him, "Yes you can!"

"There we were with him in all these braces, and he was in a big wheelchair that looked like something from the 1800s—it was higher up and more supportive than what he has now. And I'm thinking, this is so cruel," says Renee. "We barely had time to think that he was paralyzed and now they're saying, this is going to be your life, like it or not, get used to it, or you'll have all these problems. There were many days like that."

On another of those days, Cindy went with Scott to a class about bowel and bladder function. Again, he couldn't handle it. "We went back to my room, and I puked my guts out. I don't know, the whole idea of it… my nerves… it was a combination of everything. It just made me sick."

Eventually, though, Scott came to understand, "They scare the hell out of you in some ways, but they want you to be aware."

Scott was right, there are reasons for Kessler's tough love. One is the stark reality that the insurance clock is ticking. The staff simply doesn't have the luxury of easing patients into things. The other part of it, says Dr. Vocaturo, "is that we're very strong believers that knowledge is very empowering. We want to give people as much information as we can about their new bodies as quickly as possible, so they can start to be masters of their own bodies and be proactive. We understand that, for many patients, it's just another representation of their loss of control and loss of power. But our message is also that they can still have a quality of life even though they have to do things differently than they did before."

In spite of the sensory overload that Scott felt and the angst he unloaded on friends and family, Dr. Vocaturo isn't surprised that his response to physical and occupational therapy was just the opposite. "We don't typically see patients breaking down or getting tearful while they're participating in therapy. That's where we're able to focus on their recovery and rehabilitation. That's a place where they're getting better or they're working on getting better."

Upbeat is just how physical therapist Barb Garrett and occupational therapist Gabriella Steifbolt remember Scott. "He was pretty bad in terms of his injuries," Barb recalls, "but right from the start, he had a strength within and tried so hard not to give in to the pain. He knew he had a wife and kids to get back to. He would talk about his work and wonder what capacity he could get back to that. It wasn't, 'I'm defeated by this.' It was, 'How am I going to get past this and get back to my life?' I remember that. He would talk about the kind of work he was doing and I would ask a lot of questions, because I don't know much about lumber."

As the days ticked by, the old Scott started peeking through, and he began joking around. For Barb, he was the "fun kind of patient"—the kind who was "eager to get back, and focused, but with a good sense of humor. We'd joke about things, and one time he told me how to get rid of my poison ivy. You figure he's someone who knows trees—I got so itchy and he told me to put bleach on it. He's *such* a lumberjack. Now, every time I get poison ivy, I think of him. That's a neat person who can look beyond what they're going through and joke with you. That's what's cool about him."

Gabriella also found that Scott had an extremely high tolerance for pain. "We knew he was in pain, so we tried to work on things to address it. Sometimes it might be strengthening in a different position or maybe doing something a different day if we were working on a tougher skill. But he really was a good sport about it. He tried not to give in."

All the while, Scott worked like a dog. Some days, skidding trees out of a dense forest on steep terrain seemed like a walk in the park compared to learning to sit up straight, propel his wheelchair, get dressed, shift his weight, and regain enough upper body strength to transfer himself from place to place—there were special, separate maneuvers for chair-to-shower, chair-to-toilet, chair-to-couch, chair-to-bed, and so on and back again. With his incisions and bones still raw, the transfers were killers. "Everything hurt, so all I felt was pain," he says. "There was a lot of times I was trying and the sweat was running down my face, and I felt like I was gonna pass out. But they pushed me."

Because of his work ethic, Gabriella says, "he's someone you remember. You remember who he was. Hard-working patients like that—you don't forget them." For quite a while after his discharge, Scott would send Barb and Gabriella pictures of himself on his snowmobile with the wheelchair hanging on the back, and on his all-terrain vehicle. Gabriella keeps them in her office and loves showing them to other patients. "It's nice to be able to say, 'See, you can do a lot of things when you leave here. Here's somebody who's similar to your level and here's what he did.' He probably doesn't realize what he's done for people who have come after him."

Scott talks about Barb, Gabriella, and Dr. Benevento with warmth and reverence; yet, as with students everywhere, some of his most valuable education did not come from the classroom, and his best teachers were not only the pros. Scott's new vision of himself and the world, and his nascent understanding of what it meant to live in a spinal cord injured body, were also being shaped by the sights and conversations and relationships swirling around him.

"If you could see what I saw when I was down there," he says. "I started to see that there are a lot of people who are worse off than me. You see a kid come in, fourteen years old, paralyzed from the neck down. It's so sad. And you're sitting there saying to yourself, 'You got life bad? Look at that poor girl. What is she gonna be able to experience in her life?'" He forged his first relationships with people who knew firsthand what tough luck was all about.

"There were four of us in our room." One young man, Chris, who had been injured when he was twenty, was twenty-five when Scott met him. He had been at Kessler for a year with a bedsore. "He had no use of his hands, had to use his mouth for everything. He got hurt in a diving accident. And this guy, if you want to look up to somebody, he'd be that somebody. That kid... He could give you the strength to go on. He was allowed out of his bed fifteen minutes a day. Can you imagine?"

The roommates shared the camaraderie of veteran soldiers who had fought in different wars. Joe Rizzi, a graphic artist, was one of them. He had been a fit and healthy fifty-year-old when he developed a staph infection—no one can tell him how it happened or how long he had had it—but it caused an abscess on his cervical spine that squeezed his cord at C5. After a weekend of yard work, he developed pain that felt like he had pulled a muscle. After a visit to the doctor, X-rays from an orthopedist, and a trip to the chiropractor, it continued to worsen, until, by the following Saturday night, he was pacing his house unable to sleep from the pain that zinged through his body. By the early hours of Sunday morning, with his legs tingling, he sat down on a kitchen chair, and "Boom!" he says. "Everything shut down. I couldn't move."

Joe remembers that both he and Scott had great support from family and friends. Their wives got to meet and talk and commiserate. In fact, both Joe and his wife marveled at Cindy. "She was gung-ho like you wouldn't believe. My wife had moments when she was angry and crying and wondering why this happened. But Cindy was rah, rah, rah, let's go."

To Barb Mullaney, whose eighteen-year-old son Buddy was another of Scott's roommates, the Cindy-Scott combination was a godsend. Buddy was days away from leaving for the air force, when he went out with friends and was paralyzed in a car accident. Buddy had been a back seat passenger. The driver was killed. "Buddy had a very hard time when he got [to Kessler]. He was very emotional," Barb remembers. "Scott and his wife took Bud under their wings. They really did. They would talk to him and boost him up and yell at him about his attitude. Buddy wouldn't talk to me much, but Scott and Cindy would pull me aside and tell me how his days went. Him and his wife were like the mother and father whenever we weren't there."

Barb called Buddy and Scott "the rebels," because they were both so determined, independent, and headstrong, and they both hated the Kessler food, absolutely wouldn't eat it some days. So Barb and Cindy did a lot of food runs, and that gave them a chance to "talk like friends." "I had it rough," Barb admits, "and I know Cindy took it rough, too, but she was there for him." Barb also remembers how amazed she was at the support Cindy and Scott got from their town. "I'll tell you," she says, "That town! The money they got, Cindy didn't know what to do with it all. They even talked about buying a special wheelchair for Buddy, but in the end, we did get insurance. But I remember that they felt very funny taking from people."

Still, people gave and gave.

With the money Cindy got from the community, the family was able to rent the top floor apartment in a two-family house in West Orange. Renee and Cindy were fixtures at Kessler, spelling each other when one or the other would have to run back home to take care of business or bring other family members down. Renee, who quit her job to be with Scott, had bought a new car three weeks before his accident. By the end of that summer, the odometer read 21,000 miles.

True to form, the other members of the family camped out with them in a continuous round robin. When school let out, Renee's daughter, Joss-Elyse, spent most of the summer in New Jersey, hanging out with John Roscoe and Jenna, and being one of Scott's most ardent cheerleaders.

Scott was more than an uncle to Joss, who was eleven at the time. He was one of her best friends. "We just always had a lot of fun with each other," she says. "I can talk to him about anything, like boys or anything. He always goes, 'Who are you with this week?' And we just joke around. We're really, really tight." Joss just wanted to be near Scott, and she wanted to be there for her cousins and keep them entertained. She got friendly with the family living next door to the apartment, and they let her swim in their pool with little John and Jenna. She would also go with her cousins to Kessler to visit Scott, where John continued to be extremely quiet, although he loved to sit with Scott's roommate, Chris, and watch baseball. Jenna, on the other hand, wanted the low-down on everything, sometimes donning a pair of rubber gloves that Dr. Benevento had given her and helping Dr. Benevento check up on her other patients.

Gert spent so much time at Kessler, she figured she might as well volunteer. So she regularly wheeled patients to meals and therapy sessions, and, not surprisingly, still keeps in touch with many of them.

Chris Johnson couldn't make it down to New Jersey, but his phone calls, once or twice a week like clockwork, were among Scott's sweetest diversions. "Sometimes we talked about what was going on down there," says Chris, "but mostly we just talked. Talked about NASCAR and what was going on back home."

Scott's cousin, Bud DeMatties, who had spent all those Huck Finn summers with the Remingtons, was now a fire investigator, and got to see Scott at Kessler on several occasions while traveling on business. Those conversations surprised Bud: "I was amazed and sort of taken aback, but at the same time, I had a feeling of pride about the things he was realizing. It's not that I saw a sense of maturity, because I don't think he was an immature person," but Bud was struck by the fact that, in such a short time and in the wake of such a life-altering event, Scott seemed to be thinking on a whole new level.

In one conversation, Scott admitted to Bud his worry that Cindy didn't seem to be unloading on anyone about the accident, not to him or Renee or anyone he knew of. Both Cindy and Renee were equally gung-ho when it came to boosting Scott's spirits and pitching in to help, but Renee was talking to everyone about Scott, and she cried continuously for and with her brother. Cindy did not. Scott was sure that she was trying to be strong for him, but, says Bud, "Scott's telling me that *he's* talked to the psychologist, and he was telling me, 'She's not letting down to me,' and he recognized that it was bad for them and for her.

"You've got to remember who you're getting all this from," he adds. "This is from a woodsman. He's like the kind of guys you read about in storybooks who don't believe in talking to a psychologist. They don't do things like that. By the time I really had an in-depth conversation with him at Kessler, I was amazed at the transformation I was seeing. I was seeing a guy who knew he was gonna need help and who knew his wife was gonna need that. I mean, not knew it like mentioning it casually, but genuinely concerned *already* that they would need help if they were going to survive. It was like talking to someone who'd been prejudiced and now they're not."

Bud saw the transformation, too, when Scott said about his family, "Y'know I have to find a way to have them back off me." In particular, Scott mentioned that the family and hospital staff had been pushing him to eat more.

Bud assured Scott, "They're worried that you're not recovering and that you're not gaining your strength."

"I understand that," said Scott, "but they don't understand, and it doesn't help me to explain to them that my wife has to be able to move me. I'm not saying I've got to get skinny. I'm not losing weight to the point where I'm gonna be sick, but I can't weigh two hundred pounds when I go home. I just want to take control of myself because I don't want to get to the point where I can't get the help I need."

What really touched Bud, though, was that Scott seemed to be changing before his eyes, while still hanging onto his old self. Scott's doctors were not just fixated on how he was faring there at Kessler, but also at how he would manage on the outside. For instance, they would not allow him to go home until he had an accessible place to live, even if it meant moving into an interim facility while his house was being renovated. When the staff heard that Scott's log home was on three levels and that his bedroom was in a loft, they suggested that he move. Scott relayed this all to Bud in a swirl of worry, sadness, and annoyance.

"Look Scott," Bud said, "that's something they can't do. You decide what you want to do and we'll make it happen, whatever we have to do. In your condition, your home is gonna be a big part of you. It's crazy for you to even think about going where you don't want to be." Bud thinks that Scott just needed to hear from someone what he was already thinking. "He thought about moving for maybe a half a second. It was that quick. I don't think he ever questioned that he'd go home again."

No one else questioned it either. Scott's house would require considerable modification, but Renee and her husband, John, thought that their place could be modified quickly to give Scott and Cindy the stopover they needed. "Renee and I talked about it," says John. "And we knew a carpenter who we thought could jump right on it, and he did, thank goodness. We made the bathroom bigger, took out our vanity, put in a handicapped toilet, and put in a ramp." They would switch houses with Scott and Cindy until Scott could get into his own home.

Scott's home wasn't the only hurdle he had to clear to be discharged. Scott and Cindy would have to spend one weekend alone in Kessler's mock apartment, making sure that they could handle cooking, laundry, bathing, and bowel and bladder regimens without help. They were also encouraged to go out on day passes and begin to taste the world. Scott wanted to go to a restaurant and eat real food, so Cindy and Gert took him to TGI Friday's one night in West Orange. Scott quickly discovered that reentry into the world would be trickier than he thought.

When they got to Friday's, it was packed, and Scott froze. Having to be in the wheelchair and still bound into his body and neck braces, he just couldn't go in. Everyone would stare and he couldn't stand the thought. Cindy and Gert tried to change his mind. "What do we care?" they said. "You can't hide behind this the rest of your life." But Scott couldn't make himself budge. Cindy finally went in to order take-out. Scott sat in the car with Gert, staring into the windows of the busy restaurant, saying over and over, "I really want to go in." It was like standing on the edge of a dock, wanting desperately to swim with the other kids, but unable to make your body take the freezing plunge. Cindy came out and said that the order would be ready in twenty minutes.

Just then, Gert noticed some people get up and leave a table in the back corner of the restaurant. She suggested that Cindy go back in and ask the waitress if she would hold the table for a few minutes, and she turned to Scott and said that if they sat at that table, he could sit with his back to everyone. He gave in. The three went in single file with Cindy pushing Scott's chair and Gert walking close in front trying to shield Scott as much as she could.

It's just impossible to explain why or how you get flooded with emotions you can't seem to control, but Scott just remembers, "I was absolutely terrified. Of course, everyone was looking at me. I had that plastic thing on. I don't know—the reaction of the public around me. And I just wanted to say, 'It's not me!'" In the end, Scott was proud that he had managed to jump into the water, but he couldn't get out of there fast enough.

Nor could he get home fast enough. He was chomping at the bit, and, in reality, by the end of July, he had reached a rehab plateau. Later, when he was free of the body brace, he would be able to return for more occupational therapy, primarily to relearn to drive. For now, though, there was no reason not to let him go.

The rest of the family went back home, and, on July 29, 1999, he and Cindy packed his belongings. Scott made the rounds, saying good-bye to the friends, therapists, and doctors who had helped him come so far. Then, as Kessler shrank into the rearview mirror, Scott was sure of just one thing: He was dying to move on.

Everything else was not so clear.

Kessler does what it can to prepare patients physically and psychologically for home. The staff encourages patients to test-drive the real world. They require patients to make it through a whole weekend in the on-site apartment. They coach patients on new ways to move and eat and do laundry and have sex. They are unstinting in exposing patients to potential perils that await them if they don't take care of their bodies. But Kessler is *not* the real world. "Kessler is designed for people in wheelchairs," says Dr. Vocaturo. "Kessler is designed for the disabled population. It's a very sheltered, safe environment. The world out there is not like the world at Kessler."

Undated photo of Scott, the young logger.

Scott, in the passenger seat, cruising with childhood friends: Bob Peck (driving), and in the truck bed, cousin Jimmy Remington (foreground) and Jim Peck.

Scott, the star high school soccer player, seen here disrupting an opponent's moves, showed no fear on the field.

In 1981, Scott, 10th grade, and sister Renee, 11th grade, were inseparable.

Fresh kill, three deer and two black bears, hanging from the façade of Scott's Remington Logging garage, waiting until Scott and friends could get together for a butchering party.

Scott (left) mugging on the dance floor at his wedding with
best friend and best man Chris Johnson. Chris was so much
a part of the Remington family that Gert called him "my
number six."

In 1996, young John and Jenna Remington pose in their dad's new pulp truck. Scott had bought his dad and uncle's logging business in 1993.

Portrait of John "Bull" and Gertrude Remington taking in 2001 to mark their 65th birthdays.

Scott and Trish Jarvis-Weber on Scott's deck. Scott couldn't believe how easy it was to talk to Trish and how much it changed his life to have a true friend who knew, first hand, what his life felt like.

Slowly but surely, through his own guts and determination
and the relentless support of family and friends, Scott reclaims
what he loves – riding a waverunner, driving his "mule", riding
a snowmobile with his wheelchair hanging off the back, and
hunting.

Thanksgiving 2002. Front row, left to right: Adrian and Dakota, Stephanie and Keith's children; Jenna and John. Second row seated, left to right: Renee, Joss-Elyse, Scott, and Scott's friend Bill Strauss. Standing from left to right: Renee's husband John Smith; Angie, a friend of Denise; Jeffrey, Denise's son; Stephanie; Jeremy, Denise's son; Denise; Stephanie's husband Keith Wood; Denise's husband Bill McGlashan; and Bull.

Nick deGregory faithfully tends bar at every one of Scott's fundraisers.

Gert and Earle flank the Albany River Rat hockey mascot at the third fundraiser.

Ed "Mr. PR" Jay (left), Wendy Meade, and David Carmel, the night before the fourth fundraiser in 2003, when David's brother, Dr. Jason Carmel, spoke to the fundraiser committee and members of the community on spinal cord research.

The 2002 Chiefs. With Scott and the team are co-coach Steve Bureau (back row first on left), his son Steve Jr. (back row 5th from left), co-coach Karl Dingman (back row second from right) and his son Noah (front row 4th from left). Jenna is sitting on the arm of Scott's wheelchair and John "Roscoe" is in the back next to Coach Bureau.

John "Roscoe" Remington proudly poses with his first solo kill in the winter of 2003.

Jenna Remington poses in Scott's driveway with her BB gun.

Living a dream. In February 2004, Scott was shocked when
he was invited to visit Christopher Reeve at his home for
a personal chat. Renee and John, who accompanied him,
said Scott was a nervous wreck driving to the actor's home.
But Christopher put them at perfect ease and spent two
"unbelievable" hours with them. On Friday, October 29, 2004,
Scott and Renee were deeply honored to be among the invited
guests at the memorial service for Christopher in New York
City.

10.

Home sweet unknown

Heading north up the New York Thruway, the congestion of the New Jersey/New York Metropolitan corridor gradually gives way to the wooded landscape of upstate. You can expect a spurt of traffic volume around Albany and perhaps Saratoga Springs, but after that, you're pretty much home free.

With every mile, Scott and Cindy moved closer to the heart. Signs along the way morphed from letters on green metal to names that packed more and more emotional punch. Scott, now passenger rather than driver, stared out the window as they traversed the Hudson River watershed, passing Woodstock then Saugerties. Around Kingston, the airbrushed image of distant mountains came into sight along with creeks and mountains named Plattekill, Sawkill, and Catskill. After the highway split, where I-90 sends traffic toward Buffalo or Montreal, the I-87 Thruway sucked them deeper into his life's emotional vortex. They passed Lake George, Glens Falls,

159

Warrensburg, Bolton Landing, and the sign that tells travelers that they're "Entering Adirondack Park: A six-million acre state park of public and private land"—the point at which all roadside advertising disappears, and you look up and swear that the highway is headed straight into a wall of soft-humped mountains—and Scott felt his pulse racing. Finally turning off at Exit 25 Brant Lake, they made the right turn onto Route 8 and crossed the little bridge over Schroon River with its reddish metal arches, past the Countryside Diner, and on toward town.

Then, on the right, Scott caught sight of the Remington Logging garage. *His* garage, with the lineup of antlers that Jimmy had collected over the years nailed along the top of the façade, and with the post jutting out from the side of the building where he and his posse used to hang fresh kill. With all his trucks and equipment sitting idle, the physical evidence of his working life was shut down tight. The tears started, and he couldn't stop them.

"It was devastating seeing all my equipment sitting there at the garage, not being run. When I came into town, I just cried." Stopping at the house before moving in to Renee and John's, "I was even more upset. There's my pickup—an extended-cab, teal blue Silverado; God, I loved that truck; what a beauty—and the snowmobile. Looks like your whole life is, y'know, just sitting there. And I can't get up the stairs in the house. And I just cried. Here you were a businessman, on top of your life, feeling great about yourself. Y'know, life's going well, when all of a sudden, you're wondering what you're gonna do and who you are. You lose your work, you lose your identify in some respect. You don't know what's gonna happen next, and if you can provide for the family. What are you worth?

Before, you knew how everything was, then coming home, you're wondering how everything is gonna be. It runs a lot through your mind. I sat and cried to Cindy, and said I didn't want to go on. She said, 'You gotta fight! C'mon, you got two kids. Fight, fight, fight, and you keep fighting.'"

Yet the trip into town, up to the house, and on to Renee's also came with a warm surprise. The town was awash in blue ribbons. They had stayed up all that time that he was away, and they were everywhere, including on his own mailbox.

Gert had had a similar sensation. When Scott had been discharged from Burlington, she headed home for the first time since the accident, before going down to Kessler. Entering town from the head of the lake, she was touched to see a little blue ribbon on a mailbox. Then, there was another and another. "I'm telling you," she says, "I come through town and I heard that there were ribbons in all three towns [Brant Lake, Chestertown, Pottersville], but you just can't imagine—on mailboxes, on doors, on light posts. Then I saw a neighbor, I don't even know the woman, don't know her name or anything about her, and she had blue ribbons on her door. I lost it. I cried."

Scott was home but not home. Every reason to rejoice and relax was challenged by a reminder that he was not going to pick up where he left off. Seeing friends had always been his surefire way to let off steam and recharge his batteries, but what do you do when you're afraid to be seen? He had promised Chris Johnson that he'd call as soon as he got home, but he couldn't pick up the phone. A few days went by. Chris knew that Scott was home, and it was weird that he hadn't called, but Chris knew it was a rough time, and that "it was hard for him to get back out amongst everybody." So Chris did what brothers do, he just went on over there.

It was rough for most everyone. Wendy Meade remembers that "some people couldn't handle it." Her husband Ted agrees, "They were just nervous about seeing him." It was so awkward. What do you say? How long do you stay? But Ted and Wendy knew they had to do it. "We heard he was home, and we just went over," she says. "We just said we have to do it, so let's just do it."

Some friends and relatives hung back only because they wanted to give him space. Chris and Ed Jay were a case in point. "We left it more to the immediate family to see him at first," says Ed.

"Plus," adds Chris, "I really felt that he needed to get settled. For him to have company constantly and he's trying to work out his life."

Ed and Chris called all the time, but, says Ed, "we left it up to him as to when he wanted to have people around. We let him know if he needed anything, we were there for anything that he wanted, if he needed to spend some time with Cindy, we'd take the kids. We were available to take the kids if there was anything he needed to do."

Doing what he needed to do often required a push. Chris and his girlfriend, Lynn, told Scott and Cindy that they should all get out together for a bite to eat. Scott really wanted to go and he was all for it, but when Chris and Lynn got to the house, Scott caved. "I just can't do it," he told them. Chris, Lynn, and Cindy pressed him, finally convincing him to give it a try. "It was so hard for him to get back in the public eye," Chris remembers. "He finally did go, and I think he had a good time and maybe things started getting a little easier after that. It finally just got to a point where we just took him and started getting him out."

Little by little, people started coming around. And the help just kept coming. "We didn't stay when we went over," cousin Chris Jay explains, "but I took meals over all the time." She was typical. There was a constant flow of food. Ramps began appearing at house after house after house so that Scott could regain access to his world. Later, when Scott was driving again, he and Roger Daby down at the general store figured out a new routine. Since the general store building is antique, it couldn't be fitted with a ramp. "It's not their fault," Scott understands. "So Roger said, 'Just drive up and blow the horn.' And that's what I do, just blow the horn or shout to them, and they bring stuff out to me."

Meanwhile, Gert and Bull were getting busy on their house. "Guess you could say my mom's house is… cluttered," Denise offers diplomatically. "They had some rearranging to do."

And the building crew kicked in.

Scott was dying to get back into his own house, but that was impossible in its current state. Even before he was discharged from Kessler, his caseworker, Toni, had jumped into action, getting architects in there to look the place over, rounding up quotes for the insurance company, and securing the funds to install an elevator and build a new master bedroom and bath.

Of course, no one connected to the Remingtons was about to let strangers take on something like that. Scott's house became a community project with two clear objectives—get it done fast and stretch the dollars as far as they can go. Work got underway during hunting season of 1999. Family friend Bryce Johnson remembers that "one of the guys who hunts in our party is a contractor and he kind of oversaw the project. A bunch of us got together and went up and got the framework all closed in for him. Wintertime was coming along. I happened to be on vacation, and I think I probably worked a week and a half, two weeks, and it was just complete enjoyment for me. It really was. They're not only a good group of guys to hunt with, but if you get in a situation such as this, God, we just had a great time working together. I always hear tell of when, if a neighbor's barn burnt down, everybody in the neighborhood got together and went over, and the wives all cooked, and the men had a barn raising or house raising or whatever the occasion happened to be. This is really what it felt like to me."

Roger Daby was another one. "I just knew they were doing work up there, and when I had time, I just went up and helped out. Everybody knew what was going on, so we helped out whenever we could."

As soon as his friends had built a ramp into Scott's house, but before the addition was barely started, Scott couldn't wait to be back in his own place. Cindy, he sensed, wasn't in such a hurry. "I'm thinking maybe it bothered her some. Maybe it was knowing how everything was before, then coming home and wondering how everything is gonna be now. I know there's so many emotions that go through you."

But he and Cindy did go back to the log home tucked into the hill that they had built together. They slept in their son's tiny bedroom, while the new master suite was under construction. And when it was all finished, they warmed the place with a big party to celebrate with friends and family and thank everyone who had had a hand in the renovation. "We were all invited," says Bryce. "Everybody got together and had food, and games to play. Just a plain, good get-together."

Even Steve Satterfield, Scott's friend from Finch, Pruyn, who had driven Cindy to the hospital in Burlington, was there. He chatted with Scott about how Scott could stay active in the logging business by keeping his pulp truck on the road and hiring drivers to haul timber for other loggers in the area. Knowing Scott's love for the business, Steve says, "I tried to steer him that way."

In the head games that followed Scott's accident, the whole idea of "help" became a new source of confusion and mixed emotions. He and Cindy were grateful beyond words for the flood of support, but they were also both fiercely independent, self-sufficient people. It was hard to reconcile the constant attention and flow of offers, and equally hard to admit that they needed help. The assistance that made their new life easier was sometimes a source of tension at home, where it was a strain to get through each day.

Scott was still forced to wear the plastic body brace, although at least it looked a bit less ominous since John and Jenna had covered the thing with stickers. Scott also continued to be wracked with pain, and just getting out of bed made him feel like his body was breaking apart. Cindy was managing the kids and the house and helping Scott with dressing, bathing, bowel and bladder programs, and medication. Meanwhile, the Remingtons, driven by love and concern, were a constant presence in their lives. Renee continued to devote her time and energy to Scott, and she and Bull helped to drive Scott to therapy and doctors' appointments, and—along with other friends and family members—pitched in constantly.

Still, Scott's caseworker, Toni, who checked up on Scott regularly, thought it was obvious that Scott and Cindy needed more help at home. Cindy, she thought, was clearly in charge and doing a remarkable job, but, Toni remembers, "I wanted her to take a little break. By that I mean, get people in there to help. I got the insurance company to offer all kinds of services, like home health aides and people to come into the home to provide respite." But Cindy was a doer and highly protective of whatever privacy she and Scott could maintain. "It's just how they wanted to handle it," says Toni, "but when there's a trauma case like this, you just need some rest period."

Physical therapy sessions, which Scott started within days of returning home, promised a modicum of relief for Cindy, because therapy also promised more control for Scott. On top of everything, Cindy was now working full-time at the post office, and Scott was struggling with the restrictions of the body brace and a rental wheelchair that was bulkier than the sport model he had graduated to at Kessler.

In spite of his limitations, Scott initially reported to his therapists that he was doing a pretty good job dressing himself, using a technique where he lay supine on the bed. He was also managing to bathe himself, albeit with Cindy's help. The bathroom at Renee's and the one he used at home before the addition was finished had bathtubs. In both cases, the toilet was opposite the tub, too far away to transfer straight from toilet to tub bench. Being so physically weak and still suffering the pain of his broken ribs, Scott needed Cindy to help him get from his wheelchair to the toilet, where they were still working to program his body to void every morning, then back to the wheelchair and onto the tub bench. His new accessible bathroom would have a wheel-in shower that would allow him to go from toilet to shower on a mobile shower seat.

He was willing to put these ancillary issues of bathroom transfers and other tasks of daily life on the back burner, though, in order to devote time to one primary objective. He was clear on what he wanted above all else, and one of his therapy reports reflects that. Under "Patient's Goals" just one item appears: "The patient states that his goals [stet] for occupational therapy is to become more independent with his bowel program." The report goes on to explain, "The patient's wife assists with digital stimulation daily secondary to the patient's difficulty positioning using his existing commode. More specifically, the patient has difficulty maintaining his balance when attempting to perform digital stimulation… Scott wishes to attempt different techniques prior (to) the next occupational therapy session."

"… to become more independent with his bowel program." Honestly, when what you want is to feel whole, what else is there?

So his therapists worked on different techniques and offered him some assistive devices to try. Then August 30 brought a major step forward, when his surgeon okayed the removal of the body brace. For the first time in months, Scott was able to sit upright without being encased in plastic. Freedom from the brace was the ticket that he needed to take his therapy to a new level and really start to rediscover his sense of balance, his upper body strength, and the range of motion that he needed to take care of his most basic needs.

That trip to the surgeon, though, didn't bring entirely good news for Scott. After follow-up X-rays, Scott met the doctor in his office and asked him, as he asked every health care provider in his life, if there was a chance that he would walk again. "He just told me, 'Face it. You're not walking. Never.' Everybody else had kind of gone around the subject, but he was blunt, direct, to-the-point. I guess that was really the first time that I faced that possibility."

Scott and Cindy had been planning to turn that doctor's visit into a getaway and spend the night in Vermont. Instead, Scott just wanted to be home. He was depressed, and he was sure that he was developing a urinary tract infection—he was feeling sick and chilled. "It was a quiet ride home. I wanted Cindy to turn up the heat in the car, 'cause I kept getting chills, but she was hot. We pretty much just rode home in silence."

Still, freedom from the body jacket also made it possible to take a week in September to return to Kessler with Cindy, where he could do some advanced therapy in the pool and, most importantly, re-learn to drive.

West Orange, in New Jersey's Essex County, may be a suburb with houses and green lawns, but Mayberry it's not. Within shouting distance of New York City, lots of area residents work and play in "the City," and you can see the New York influence on the streets of this busy, often congested suburb. Getting the hang of driving with hand controls through West Orange was *some* rite of passage. Scott's a NASCAR lover and snowmobile daredevil, but, "Oh man, that was hairy," is all he can say.

Scott also tested life that week, when he took an overnight pass from Kessler and went to Atlantic City with Cindy and a couple Viagra in his pocket. Cindy drove Scott's new Ram pickup, which was not yet retrofitted with hand controls, and Scott was dazzled when they pulled into the opulent Trump Plaza. They did some gambling and had fun seeing the sights, and before heading out for dinner that night, Scott popped a pill. "A rehab doctor I saw when I got home prescribed the Viagra. I was taking it for the first time, and I'm figuring we're gonna have a great night. But we're sitting there eating at this really nice restaurant, and all of a sudden I'm getting dizzy. I don't know what's going on. I don't know if it was the combination of other pain medication or what, but I start to feel really sick, and I said, 'Cindy, we gotta get going.'"

Cindy grabbed the waiter, paid the bill, and got Scott back to their room. "We didn't end up doing anything. I went to bed. I felt terrible. It was frustrating and embarrassing. Here I wanted to go to it, and it's my first time trying the stuff, and I'm just sick. I don't even know if it ever did its thing."

Scott came home for good from Kessler on October 1, and three days later resumed three-day-a-week therapy sessions in Glens Falls, and this time he lucked out with just the taskmaster he needed. He cursed Esther Halden at times, but, like so many people with whom he crossed paths, he ultimately came to call Esther a friend, and knows full well what she has meant to his life.

At the time, Esther was a staff physical therapist at Glens Falls Hospital, with a heavy caseload in neurological patients—people with spinal cord and brain injuries and strokes. When she first met Scott, she remembers that, "He required assistance with pretty much everything. He wasn't pushing his wheelchair very far. He couldn't get from his wheelchair to a bed without help. Basically, we started on a program to try to control his pain and teach him how to move."

Three times a week for the next couple of months, Esther worked with Scott to help him move through pain and weakness. Because they kept in touch long after their sessions stopped, she knows that it took a couple of years before he was—for all intents and purposes—free of constant pain, but she pushed him hard. "Pain does some funny things to you," she says. "You try so hard not to move, but when you do move, it helps the circulation and it helps the joint fluids move properly to reduce the pain. So I tried to teach him how to move and different rotational exercises and positional exercises to try to reduce some of the pain." But sometimes, she admits, she just had to tell him, "Listen, you *have* to work through it, or you're not going to be able to move."

Initially, Scott was very quiet. In one of her initial reports on him, Esther noted, as to his mental status, "The patient is alert and fairly pleasant. However, he only speaks when spoken to and has minimal initiation at the time of this evaluation." He did what he had to do and little extra. Esther knew that "he was dealing with wounds that go a lot deeper than the physical. He went from being the provider and the person who did all the physical labor to someone who couldn't even go to the bathroom by himself. He had a really hard time with that. I can't say that he opened up about it, but I think that toward the end of his therapy sessions, he got to see that he could do more for himself, and he started to take some pride in what he could accomplish."

Making Scott independent also required family meetings. Esther had to make sure that she, Cindy, and Scott were all on the same page. "When you see his wife pushing him in the wheelchair on his way to appointments," Esther says, "you have to say, 'We have a contradiction here.'" It was very tough love all around, but, from a rehabilitation perspective, there is no alternative. "You really have to push a patient to his limits. Had we not done that, Scott would still be sitting in bed and not driving a car, and not going out four-wheeling or snowmobiling."

After improving his strength and range of motion, Esther pulled out the big guns—challenging Scott to get on and off the floor and go up and down stairs. She also took him out to the parking lot and made him get in and out of her Jeep Wrangler and a friend's Ford Explorer. "I just really pushed his every capability because I knew that his goals were to get back in the woods. So we tried to simulate different things and try out different vehicles."

"You can talk to Scott," she says straight out. "He'll tell you we went head-to-head over some things. Transferring to the Jeep, he fought tooth and nail: 'I'm never gonna do this. There's no reason to do this. It's hard and it hurts. I'm just gonna have a truck with a lift.' And I said, 'Fine. You can do that, but I want you to know that you have options.'

And when he finally succeeded, he was like, 'Oh my gosh! I never thought I could do this!'"

In the two months they spent together, Esther believes that "Scott did some great things, but that is my expectation of every patient that comes through my door. Once they move past the devastation of the fact that they can't walk, they discover that, y'know what, to live my life, I don't need to walk. There's a lot I can do from a seated position." But getting to that epiphany generally requires busting through a wall of anger. Or, as Esther sees it, "tapping the anger and using that energy."

For Scott it was hard, very hard. "And it's hard to this day, I'm sure," Esther knows. But finding the power in your arms and torso to lift your body up off the floor, drag it up a flight of stairs, or heave it up into the cab of a Jeep was more than a physical feat. It was an awakening. It was a gift of options.

Maybe Barb Mullaney, the mother of Scott's young roommate, Bud, was onto something when she called Scott a rebel. Maybe successful rehab requires not just a gifted therapist, but the capacity to be or to become a rebel. It means rebelling against the regime change that circumstances have inflicted on your life. It's not rebelling in that you put your foot down and give up. It's that you refuse to give in, rebelling against the urge to grieve so you can admit that, yeah, maybe there are options.

11.

From all outward appearances

S cott was a social guy always, and as his cousin Bud has said, a guy who would take his shirt off for anyone. Yet a number of people noticed that he, and Cindy, too, recoiled at first from all the attention that his injury evoked.

Their friend, Jill Wilson, who, with her husband Gary, had cared for John Roscoe and Jenna when Scott was in the hospital, saw both Scott and Cindy as "very strong-willed and very independent." Jill suggested to Cindy a number of times that she might want to talk to a professional about this whole ordeal, and that she might want to get help for the kids to help them learn to deal with it. Jill remembers that, "Cindy was like, 'No, no, we talked to the priest at church.' But she really did turn down help, she was very stubborn about it. And he was, too. Scott was a very proud type of person, too. People were bringing them food and stuff, and they didn't need it. They wanted to take care of themselves. Scott's still that way. He's more self-sufficient than people who can walk."

Gert saw it, too. "He really didn't like us taking care of him. But there were so many personal needs, with the catheter and whatnot. Basically it was Renee and Cindy helping with that, and he was very embarrassed."

Likewise, after Scott learned to drive, he wanted to go alone to therapy, but a couple of times, he went down there, pulled into a handicapped space, and found that someone had parked too close to that spot, and he couldn't get out. He sat trapped in his car until his therapists could come out and help him out of the car. After that, someone always went with him.

Scott and Cindy felt annoyed at times, but it wasn't that they were ungrateful. They were guarding what was left of their private lives, and were reluctant to cede any more control over a life that felt like it was spinning way, *way* out of control. Yet, over time, one of the most profound changes in Scott was the softening of that reluctance—the budding recognition that, every now and then, it's OK to accept help, and, even more profound, it's OK to ask for it. As that recognition grew, his circle of friends and confidants expanded in ways that he never could have foreseen.

Some of his most important new relationships sprang from the epiphany he had about raising money for spinal cord research. He had been in the car with Renee. They were headed to therapy in Glens Falls, and he was thinking about the future, yet determined not to forget where he'd been. "I'm not spending the rest of my life in this wheelchair, that's all there is to it," he told his sister. "I've got to do something."

Scott remembers his thought process exactly. "I seen all those kids down there [at Kessler]. As bad as I am, there was a lot of people down there a lot worse off than I was. And I said to Renee, if I could raise some money, even if it don't help me out, maybe it could help somebody. That would be great. Who wants to see some fourteen-year-old kid paralyzed for the rest of her life? At least I got to live some of my life normal. I always want that hope that I'll walk again, but even if I never get on my feet, I hope somebody does. What if that fourteen-year-old girl never experiences sex the way it's supposed to be? Imagine having someone help you get dressed in the morning or wipe your rear-end. I don't want anybody to go through that. Maybe that girl can be walking down the aisle someday."

At that moment, he and Renee cooked up the idea of a fundraiser, and Scott vowed that, if they were lucky enough to make some money, he'd send all of it to Christopher Reeve.

Funny how events can intersect. Scott and Renee enlisted friends and family members to help them raise money for spinal cord research, without the vaguest idea of how they were going to pull that off. But they would get some unexpected encouragement from one of Scott's newest friends, Rick Davidson, co-owner with his brother John of Davidson Brothers brewpub in Glens Falls. Riding down to Glens Falls for therapy, Scott would say to his dad or whomever was driving, "Let's stop and have some lunch and a microbrew." And that's how Scott met Rick, or as Scott calls him, "the godsend."

Davidson Brothers is not your run-of-the-mill tavern. It's a Glens Falls reclamation project dreamed up by two hometown boys, who didn't have a clue how to run a restaurant, much less brew their own beer. "We never even knew anybody who *worked* in a restaurant," says Rick, but they were sick and tired of seeing their town going downhill. John's in the building materials business and, in the mid-1990s, Rick had sold concrete, handled logistics for Frito-Lay, and did a stint at Ben & Jerry's Homemade up in Vermont.

They sat around one day thinking what they could do, what kind of business they could start, "as regular people," that might inject some energy into "a community that was kinda in the doldrums." They settled on a brewpub—someplace where people could gather and have a good time—and bought a downtown building that had been empty for years, but had been the home of four failed restaurants. John kept his day job, and Rick took the plunge into the new business, first heading up to Maine where, in six days, he learned to make beer from a Portland brewmaster.

Rick will tell you, "We're the second smallest brewery in New York State. We're tiny. We're a joke." The punch line is that the business is cooking, and there are now restaurants, stores, even minor league ballparks stocking Davidson Brothers microbrews from Westchester County to the Canadian border. The business is driven by a mission that doesn't even mention beer or food. It's "To make the community a better place."

The food is great. The ales are smooth. But that mission statement, "that's our whole thing," says Rick. "We're kind of a strange place." On the cardboard carriers for their six-packs, there are friendly notes encouraging folks to visit the museum or theatre in Glens Falls. Rick gives to one local charity and event after another, so many that he's lost count. As he sees it, it's pretty simple, "When you support things that are going on in town and put messages on your packages about stuff going on around here, visitors come to town and their money goes right into the community… Yeah, we're a little different."

And Rick's a different business owner. When people stop in for a meal or a pint, he's out there. "I try to see everybody," and, more than a few times, he pulls up a chair for a chat. Like when Scott would come in with Bull or Renee or his cousin Ed. "I'd end up sitting at the table and getting no more work done the rest of the day," Rick laughs. "I'd have to have a beer with them and I was shot. We just had the greatest time."

One of those times was in the fall of 1999. Scott and Renee "just kinda brought up the idea of the fundraiser out of the blue. They said something like, 'Hey, we're gonna have this fundraiser, and we don't have much of an idea, but we want to do something. Could you maybe give us a $20 gift certificate we can raffle off?'" Rick got talking to them. He advised them to get as many people involved as they could and make sure they gave their guests things to do, like music and raffles, because "the more they get out of it, the more they'll keep coming back." Oh and by the way, he said, "Maybe we can do better than a gift certificate." When all was said and done, he gave them gift certificates, got banners to hang over the road in downtown Brant Lake, and had his friends at the local radio station promote the event.

Scott and Renee set the date for February 27, 2000, enlisted a bunch of people to help, and put the plans in motion. The goal they set for the 1st Annual Spinal Cord Research Benefit was $10,000. Pretty steep for a first-ever event in a small town, but they were thinking big. For Scott, Renee, Cindy, the rest of the Remingtons, and a contingent of friends, the plans became a positive, energizing diversion, as well as the backdrop for a wild winter and spring.

In October, Scott and Cindy celebrated their tenth anniversary. They should have been spending it on the beach in Aruba. They had been sitting on plane tickets and brochures for months and months, and it had been a heartbreaking day when they had to cash in the tickets after Scott was hurt. But Jill and Gary Wilson threw a big party. Tom and Lois McPhillips were there, and from all outward appearances, after everything that Scott and Cindy had been through, Lois can picture them perfectly that day. "I've never seen two people so in love. Especially that day, Cindy was all over him. And when we were leaving, she hugged us and said, 'Oh, this is so great.'"

Renee, too, was impressed and moved by how hard Scott and Cindy were working to rebuild their lives. At Thanksgiving, Renee gave Cindy a gold bracelet that had belonged to her husband's grandmother, along with a note that said, "You're golden. I know this isn't easy, but you're doing a fabulous job."

People also began to see Scott's signature humor coming back to life. Wendy Meade noticed that, as time went on, he just opened up about his situation more—what it felt like, what he was going through. She knew that, "There were a lot of ups and downs, a lot of emotional stuff going on. It's so hard for him sometimes." But then sometimes he'd have an accident, and announce to anyone in earshot, "I peed in my pants!"

"Scott!" Wendy would laugh. "Information overload! Y'know we don't need to know this!"

He started making fun of Gert, too. She couldn't believe how fit he was getting, and how easily he was transferring from place to place. "I can't even lift my rear end up!" she says. "I put my arms on a chair the way he does, and he pushes himself from his wheelchair to the recliner or the other way, and I can't even come up an inch! And he'd say, 'C'mon Mom, you can do it!'"

In the eyes of everyone around them, it just seemed like Scott and Cindy were finally on a roll, in fact, so much so that Renee urged them to come with John and her and a bunch of their friends on a snowmobiling trip in early February. They had made reservations for the four-day trip to St. Donat, Canada, a year ago, before Scott's accident. Racing through the back woods was a winter tradition for Scott for as long as he could remember, and getting back on a snowmobile would be an unbelievable affirmation that he could reclaim what he loved. Chris Johnson knew, too, that, "The snowmobiling was a big thing. It was something Scott really wanted to do, but he didn't know how he was gonna do it." So, together, Chris and Scott practiced near home—getting Scott on and off his machine, rigging it so he could strap his wheelchair on the back, and making sure that Scott could ride without the ability to control the lower half of his body.

All told, about a dozen people headed north to Canada to make four days of new memories…

There was the motel room with the bathroom doorway too narrow for Scott's chair, so a bunch of the guys yanked the door off its hinges. There was his friend, Kenny Higgins, drag-racing Scott across the motel parking lot. "I was running him across the parking lot in the wheelchair," Kenny remembers, laughing. "I just pushed him real fast and hung onto him so he couldn't go out. It was crazy, but that's nothing. The way he drove a snowmobile was unbelievable for a guy who's paralyzed. He scared me to death half the time."

There was the time when they came in from the woods, and access to Scott's room was blocked by some snowmobiles parked in the way. "Cindy was having a fit," Kenny recalls. "She was throwing these snowmobiles around left and right to get Scott in there." And then there was just hanging out at night, laughing and drinking.

Scott was in his element. It wasn't the same, nothing was. But for the first time in a long, long time, he just let it rip. "It hurts to drive a snowmobile," he says, "but you pop a few pills and you're good to go." And he did—more than 250 miles in two days.

As cousin Bud sees it, heading to Canada and racing that snowmobile was a lot more than a physical leap for Scott. It was an emotional breakthrough. "When you're in the situation that he is, and you're a humble person, I think it's hard to allow other people to do things for you. But yet you have to overcome that to be sure you're doing as much as you can. Just take the snowmobiling. He did what it takes to *allow* people to help him do that. Think about it—there's a lot of sacrifices that a lot of other people around him have to do. It's a cold weather environment, and they have to worry about his feet freezing and him not realizing it. They have to make sure he can get off the snowmobile and into a warm place if he has to. They have to make sure a place can accommodate Scott when they make reservations. Knowing him the way I do, I know how hard it would be to *allow* people to help you and to maybe alter what they would normally do without him feeling guilt for it. For someone with his personality, that's a huge obstacle to overcome."

Scott came home on a high, but within weeks, they would face the first fundraiser, and Scott was a wreck. Jimbo's was ready with food and supplies. Scott and his committee had blanketed the town and surrounding areas with announcements. Letters had gone out to friends, including all the new friends the Remingtons had made in Vermont and New Jersey, and letters had been mailed to businesses, many of which had also been visited in person by Scott, Renee, Wendy, or Ed. They had registered their fundraiser with the Reeve Foundation, which generously sent them copies of Christopher's first book, *Still Me*, and Dana Reeve's book, *Care Packages*, that the committee would give away as door prizes.

But the one question that was keeping Scott up at night and making his stomach churn throughout the morning of February 27th was finally answered in a big way. People came and came and came. And after they came, they stayed and stayed. With the money the fundraiser took in on beer, raffles, and direct donations to the Christopher Reeve Paralysis Foundation, the dream of raising $10,000 became a joke when they surpassed $21,000. All of it made Scott think that, "This town and these people are an amazing story, and don't forget that they had *already* given me and Cindy more than $20,000 just to help us out. That first year I had the benefit, I never had such a feeling in my life with the people showing up and the people around me."

Among the day's many touching vignettes was the hush that fell over the crowd when David Carmel, who had been hurt only weeks before Scott, delivered a speech about spinal cord research and the reasons for hope.

News of the fundraiser had also reached another contingent of local residents who came together that day. From flyers, local publicity, and word of mouth, a small group of folks with spinal cord injuries came to party. One of them was Trish Jarvis-Weber, who has a friend in Chestertown who told another friend who told Trish. She remembers that Scott was "roaming around" the crowd and someone pointed him out to her, and she approached him at one point to say, hi. True to form, he was modest and charming and instantly accessible. "We connected pretty quick," she says. "I think mainly because of our in-common thing here, in the wheelchairs. I'm sure that's what really connected us."

It was a brief, friendly exchange, but the power of just talking with someone else in his position made an imprint on Scott that would grow stronger and stronger in the months ahead.

Everyone connected to the fundraiser was left flush with the success of it all. For weeks afterward, checks continued to roll in—direct donations to the Reeve Foundation. It was hard to believe the way it had exceeded every expectation, and, almost immediately, Scott, his friends, and family began brainstorming for the next one. But first, a few months off were in order.

As with most of Scott's life, "time off" was not about laying low. As the spring approached, the family planned a trip down to Myrtle Beach, South Carolina, where Bull and Gert, and Renee and John owned time-share condos on the beach. When all the kids got off from school for spring break in April, Scott and Cindy, Renee and John, Steph and Keith, and all their kids joined Bull and Gert for some beach time.

Sand posed some interesting issues, but Scott was game. Someone would help him get the chair down the stairs to the beach and wheel him through the soft sand until he found that happy medium where it wasn't too dry or too wet. On that supportive strip, he hung out in his chair or wheeled up and down the beach for exercise. They ate at the NASCAR Café and "did all the touristy stuff," and Cindy took him to a go-cart track for some time trials. The whole family helped him get into the little, two-seater racecar, which was no small feat, because of a lip on the car that he had to get over. Cindy slipped behind the wheel and raced them both around the track. Nothing much gets to Scott, especially when it comes to speed, but he can still recall that, "Those cars were *real* fast. Scared me half to death!"

Scott had been thinking a lot about how to get back to work, but his talk with Steve Satterfield at the "renovation party" and Steve's offer to refer work to Scott, were the extra push he needed. It had been another heartbreak when Scott had sold all the equipment from Remington

Logging, but he had kept his beloved pulp truck. In January of 2001, he put the truck and the new business, Remington Enterprises, in Cindy's name so as not to jeopardize his unemployment benefits while he was getting started, and enlisted the help of his brother-in-law, Bill MacGlashan.

Scott contacted a landowner he'd worked with before who owned a large woodlot with a hunting camp in Brant Lake, and, when it came time to harvest the wood again from the lot, Scott got the job for Bill. Bill did the cutting, loaded it onto Scott's truck, and a driver who Scott had hired delivered the wood to the mills. It was a start, but it allowed him to work from home while he was still dealing with significant physical pain and the hassles of trying to master his new body. And while the new trucking company was a stripped-down version of his former business, Scott hoped that it would eventually be successful enough that he could support his family again and "get rid of all the Social Security and Worker's Comp."

For the time being, though, this toe-in-the-water was as much as Scott could handle. The whole concept of risk loomed larger than it ever had before. "I'm not so sure of myself anymore," he explains. "Before, I could go buy a sixty-, seventy-thousand dollar piece of equipment and not bat an eye, because I knew I could pay for it. Now, I'd be scared shitless, and I was, then, with the new business. But when your body don't work, and you know you can't do a hands-on thing yourself, and you need somebody else to do it for you, that's very difficult. Don't get me wrong, I was dependent on workers before. But I could always pick up the extra—y'know, do the extras if somebody wasn't there, or if we just needed an extra pair of hands. Now, I don't know, the health I'm in. You have good days and bad days. Some days you ache so." But it was a start.

Also around that time, Renee's husband, John, was nudging Scott back onto the Little League field. Scott had been coaching his kids since t-ball, but when John approached him about assisting with Joss-Elyse's team, he said to John, "I can't do that. How can I teach the kids to do this stuff now?" John told him, "Listen, Goober, you can show them how to throw. You can be my assistant coach, and since this is Joss' last year in the league, and Roscoe will be playing a few more years and Jenna will be starting, you can take over the team next year."

Scott agreed, but nothing felt right. During that first season, John remembers that Scott would look at him and say, "'Could you go out and talk to the pitcher?' He'd ask me to do this and that. He didn't want to go out and do those things, he didn't want to wheel out to the mound and talk to the pitcher. He didn't think he could do it."

In spite of constant pain, Scott was also working hard at home to get back in shape. He was working out with weights to regain muscle mass, and he'd gotten a "standing chair" so he could let his lower extremities experience the weight of his body. He was desperate to keep his leg muscles from atrophying completely. He was determined to be ready for "the cure" that he prays will come in his lifetime and that he's working so hard to expedite with his fundraisers.

Then a phone call from his friend, Kenny Higgins, that fall drew Scott even further into the world. Kenny is about ten years older than Scott, too distant in age to be friends growing up, but Kenny has known the Remingtons all his life. He lives on a 435-acre Brant Lake estate, where he has been the caretaker for nearly thirty years. He's also a guitar player, a "one-man band," as he describes himself, "who does everything from country to the modern stuff today, Neil Young, Eagles, Alabama, Credence, you name it." Over the years, he's played at a lot of Remington family parties. "Whenever they had a celebration like a birthday or anniversary, I was always asked to play."

While Scott was in the hospital and at rehab, Kenny called Cindy a few times, and he left a card in their mailbox, but it was after Scott came home that Kenny felt compelled to get in touch. He still has to control his emotions remembering the initial contact. "I knew he loved to hunt," Kenny says, then pauses, his voice shaking. "You have to wait a minute, I get a little emotional… I knew how much he loved to hunt, and I just wanted to be part of taking him. I knew how much Scott loved the woods, so I figured it would be my thing to take him. And it gave me a great feeling to be able to take him."

It wasn't like the old days. It wasn't bushwhacking through dense brush and up mountains, but it had its own, new magic. Kenny cleared a path to an old barn on the estate where he lives, so he could wheel Scott out there, "and he can watch out of the barn," Kenny explains, "where he's out of the wind, and we sit together and have some great conversations. He tells me some of his problems and we talk 'em through, and we watch for deer." Soon it became almost a nightly thing. Kenny would drive Scott into the estate, then wheel him to the barn, and almost every night they'd see some game.

One night, a doe walked into view about twenty-five yards from the barn. Scott moved to shoot, but Kenny thought he was at a bad angle. "Scott, it's not really a good shot," he advised. "Let's wait." Just then, an even larger deer walked up in front of the first one. Kenny was looking away at that moment and continued to talk. Scott had his eye locked on the second deer. He told Kenny, "Shhhh," and shot. The second deer went down and, for a second, the two hunters looked at it, not saying a word. Then Kenny grabbed the handles of Scott's chair, and pushed him out of the barn toward the animal. It was rough going across the ground, and they had to go down a little hill, so, Kenny recalls, "I tipped his wheelchair over backwards, and I was excited, and Scott was laughing and going, 'Don't dump me outta here! Don't dump me outta here!' I said, 'Don't worry, I got ya.'" Kenny wheeled Scott up to where the deer lay, gently tipped the chair forward, and Scott reached down and touched the warm hide of his game. For Kenny, "it was so nice just to see him do that."

Scott can summon up the feeling he had to this day. "Oh, it was great. I did it, y'know. Just to know I could still get a deer if I wanted. It was great having that feeling again. There's something about hunting. I don't know what it is. It's something in your blood."

That was a profound marker in Scott's new life. It helped to temper the reality he was struggling to accept. "I love hunting the way me and Kenny do it," he says, then stops, searching for the right words. "But it's different from what I did before. I used to go up over the mountains. I loved to hike that part of it—get on a nice mountain and look at the view of ponds or something. But you got to accept that a lot of things you love to do in life you can't do them no more. So you work like hell to do them differently. You got to. You *got* to. If you want to reclaim yourself some way, you do the best you can."

From all outward appearances, Scott was doing better than that. Everyone around him could barely believe it. He seemed to be doing so well, and Scott was actually letting himself believe that maybe the after-life was worth living.

Always lurking in the shadows of his mind, though, was the thought that, "You do end up losing a lot of things. In this situation, you gotta be able to take losing things you love in life."

12.

... do us part

We all have different faces that we show the world. There's nothing duplicitous about that, because they're all genuine reflections of who we are. But there is something to the notion that we tend to "put our best face forward." Or perhaps it's not so much our best face, as our most carefree face.

Behind closed doors, it can certainly be liberating and relaxing to rest our social selves and let down our guard. But the freedom we get from privacy has a price, too, because in private, we face ourselves without distractions. Behind closed doors is where truth lies waiting, and there's no avoiding it.

Scott's life, and, by extension, Cindy's life, continued to be a trip through the health care industry, a relentless rotation from primary care physician to therapist to urologist, and, for the first year, to surgeon. Scott's body and bodily functions dominated each day's agenda. His friends and family were getting bolder about dragging

Amy Montgomery

him outside himself, and Scott increasingly let himself be dragged. Outside, it was harder for Scott to fixate on himself, and that was the best kind of therapy. The happy, social face he was increasingly showing the world was genuine. At home, though, with the world at bay, reality could be harsh for both Scott and Cindy. Looking into each other's eyes often brought them face-to-face with a rush of feelings that neither one of them had bargained for.

For Scott, sleep didn't even bring a refreshing break. He was sent home from the hospital with sleep medication, but he never took it, and still refuses to take a pill to help him sleep, even though, he says, "I haven't slept well since I got hurt." Like anyone else, he gets uncomfortable lying in one position for too long, but tossing and turning when you're paralyzed becomes a big, conscious, sleep-disturbing exercise. To roll over, he has to sit up, manually cross one leg over the other, and then turn. When he first came home from the hospital, he was too sore to do that much, but even when he was feeling better and stronger, "By the time you do all that," he says with annoyance, "you're awake." And when he does manage to turn over, he's pretty much limited to his back and stomach. It hurts too much to sleep on his side.

Every morning, he'd wake from a fitful sleep only to find that consciousness came with a slap. At night, he never dreamed—and still hasn't to this day—that he was in a wheelchair. Every dream features his old walking self. That meant that, day after day after day, he would open his eyes only to find that, beside the bed, the damn chair was always there. Not to mention that, for nearly two years, it hurt like hell just to get out of bed in the morning, so he

190

came to rely on daily doses of Vioxx to help relieve the pain and stiffness from inflammation.

Food also stopped being the spontaneous pleasure that it had been. Scott's old lifestyle had stoked his body into a calorie furnace. At five-foot-nine and 190 pounds of muscle, he could pack away a lot of fuel, especially in the winter, when he was hunting, snowmobiling, or "trudging through the snow in the woods, and it's up to your knees and you're pulling the cable on the skidder." He came home from the hospital thirty pounds lighter and with an entirely new perspective on food, coffee, and alcohol. "I never had to say I can't eat this much. I never really thought about food. Now I think about it all the time. I get hungry but I'm so scared of being overweight. I try to eat one meal a day, but sometimes I have a sandwich in the middle of the day. I'm hungry, but it's always in the back of your mind, you're saying you can't eat too much. I know if I gain too much weight, how am I gonna do anything? Transfers will just be harder. I stay away from coffee, too. It runs right through me, and I can't control it that well. A couple of beers runs right through me, too. I love beer, that's the problem. I love it. But now I'm more apt to have a glass of wine or a mixed drink, 'cause it don't run through you like a six-pack."

Added to the new menu of annoyances was the problem of regulating his body temperature, a persistent issue for anyone who's paralyzed, and the higher the injury on the spinal column, the more serious the problem.

Spinal cord injury disrupts the functioning of the autonomic nervous system, which encompasses the functions that are automatic or involuntary, like breathing, heartbeat, digestion, and temperature regulation. Scott's body was no longer efficient at triggering his shivering and sweating reflexes to keep his core temperature on an even keel.

"When I first came home it was terrible, I'd get chills for no reason," Scott explains. "Even now, if I get cold, it takes me a long time to get warm, like when I'm snowmobiling, if I get myself cold, I go to bed and sleep for a while and wake up in the middle of the night shivering, freezing."

It also didn't take long for him to develop the shoulder pain that tends to be chronic for people who propel themselves in manual wheelchairs and constantly jam their shoulders into their sockets every time they transfer.

Besides his regular Vioxx, Scott's daily meds included Ditropan to calm the spasms in his bladder, and cranberry pills to help ward off bladder infections. Still, urinary tract infections hounded him repeatedly. UTIs are another constant risk with paralysis. When you're emptying your bladder with the help of a catheter, bacteria from the skin or urethra (the thin canal that carries urine from the bladder and out through the penis) can invade and infect the bladder. Many people who are paralyzed also cannot empty their bladders completely, which gives the bacteria in the urine time to grow. They might also develop UTIs as a result of constipation or an impacted bowel. As Dr. Benevento explained, everything down there is connected.

"UTIs are the *worst* thing," Scott says, wincing. "You feel like you're dying when you have those." No wonder. The grab bag of symptoms covers the gamut from fever and chills to nausea, headache, and increased spasms.

At least, a condition known as autonomic dysreflexia or AD was not among his litany of problems, but it might have been if that beech had hit him just a few vertebrae further north. "At least that's one thing I don't get, and I'm lucky there," Scott says. UTIs put people with spinal cord injuries at risk for AD, especially when their injuries are at T6 or higher. It can be triggered by an irritant below the level of injury, so bladder or bowel infection is often a culprit. When an irritation occurs below the injury site, the irritant or infection stimulates a reflex in the autonomic nervous system that constricts blood vessels and raises blood pressure. Normally, the same stimulus would cause a message to travel up the spinal column to the brain, directing the body to moderate the constriction and re-regulate the blood pressure. In the paralyzed body, the impulses that would normally travel up to the brain are blocked at the point of injury, so, without a natural "circuit breaker," the nervous system can, literally, go haywire, causing a potentially life-threatening spike in blood pressure.

Chronic, annoying, nauseating health issues on top of a barrage of everyday adjustments took their toll on Scott and Cindy.

Family and friends continued to do whatever they could to ease the burdens.

The Remingtons were there in a heartbeat to chop and stack wood for the wood furnace. As part of the home renovation, Scott had put in an oil heater, because he "didn't want Cindy to have to monkey with wood all the time," but Bull had encouraged him to keep the wood burner as well. "I don't know why," Scott says smiling. "My dad's just a wood maniac, and it does heat real nice and saves money."

Earle, Scott's sisters, and their husbands were also always pitching in to help with odd jobs around Scott's house. "I was over there cleaning the house and taking care of stuff so Cindy could work," says Renee. "When they needed light bulbs changed or the toilet unclogged, my husband and I were there." In the winter months, Wendy Meade used to pop up there to make sure the snow hadn't boxed them in. "I used to go up and shovel all the time," she says. "Cindy was at work and we'd have these heavy snowstorms, and I'd just take my shovel and walk up there."

At the same time, Scott was doggedly trying to take back the jobs that had always been his around the house. One day, Wendy turned to her father-in-law and longtime Remington friend, Bruce, and said, "Let's go up and shovel Scott and Cindy's." She knew that Scott had been out trying to plow—he had gotten a plow hitched to the front of his truck—and she figured that she and Bruce could help out with the porches and walks. "We're out front shoveling," she says laughing, "and we hear this horn honking. We look at each other and are like, 'What is *that*?' I said, 'It sounds like it's out back.'" They walked around back of the house, where they found Scott in his truck. "He'd been plowing early in the morning and got stuck! He heard us talking and just started honking and honking. Oh, he was fine. Not really concerned at all. Just figured he'd sit there and wait it out."

Denise's husband, Bill, also remembers that first winter after Scott was hurt. "The first snowfall, he went out in his chair, and he shoveled that front porch. That was the one thing that really made me think he was gonna be all right. Took his shovel and pushed it off. I don't know how long it musta taken him. I stopped over to the house, and he was so proud telling me about it. I kinda smiled and said to him, 'Hey, next time don't miss that spot.'"

In spite of constant help, offers to help, and his own valiant efforts, Scott looks back and knows that Cindy was wrung out trying to handle the house, the kids, her job, and him. He knows that the whole issue of "help" had taken on big and sometimes confusing dimensions. It was tough to sort out the conflicting emotions that came from feeling grateful and feeling needy. It was hard to have people around all the time, no matter how well-meaning they were and how much you loved them. And all of those feelings were layered on top of a general sense of fear and confusion about life, a general sense that the ground had shifted under their feet.

Yet Scott kept telling himself that, if we just hang in, things will be all right. He was also sustained by feelings of love for Cindy that were overwhelming at times. She continued to help him through "the worst stuff you can imagine, my darkest times." She was "by my side and helping me with *everything*," he says. "I don't know how to explain how much that deepened my love for her, that she would do that and keep telling me, 'You can do it.' That was love. That was my best friend."

In the before-life, Cindy and Scott had felt right at home in traditional roles. Scott was the hunter and provider. Cindy was at peace as wife and mother. Her friend, Jill Wilson, remembers when Cindy was still in high school, "All she ever wanted was to get married and have babies." That template was now shattered. And even if their new life sometimes filled them with a sense of love and devotion that was impossible to quantify, the new life could also turn on them in a heartbeat.

Being at home during the day was not how Scott wanted his life to play out. So, when Cindy started asking him to pitch in around the house, sometimes his frustration and physical pain collided in outbursts of resentment. Now, he lowers his head when he recalls those times and is filled with regret. And it's funny how one day and one outburst, in particular, stays with him, almost as a symbol of all those days and all those feelings. In the abstract, it seems like such a little thing—laundry—but when he talks about this chapter in their lives, he always comes around to that one moment and that one conversation about the goddamn laundry, and he'd do anything to take it back.

"The day I told her I wasn't gonna do the laundry..." The half sentence just hangs in the air. In recounting the day, Scott props his elbows on the table in front of him, puts his head in his hands, and waits a second to compose himself, fighting back a tear lodged in the corner of his eye. "That was not a good idea. I shouldn't have said it. I don't know. She didn't think I was helping out enough, and I was mad. So I said, 'I didn't do laundry before, I'm not doing it now!' I didn't *feel* like being at home doing laundry. I felt like, y'know, I wasn't worth nothing. But I'm not making excuses for myself, because I never shoulda said that. And now I look at my life, and I do laundry all the time. I cook and keep my house clean—takes me *forever* to push the

vacuum around and dust stuff, what I can reach anyway—
and it makes me feel good that I'm doing it for me and for
my children. I actually do have different ideas now. But
back then, I was pissed off. I felt angry. I remember that
day. It was like, no, I don't want to do *none* of this stuff. I
want to get back on my feet. I want to *do* something."

Scott and Cindy had had a good marriage. They
butted heads now and then—Scott worked long hours in a
dangerous profession, and he loved more than anything to
have his time in the woods with the boys. There was usually
one time every hunting season when he'd stay in the woods
for a week at a stretch or over several consecutive weekends.
It was Scott's favorite form of release, something he looked
forward to all year, but it was alone time for Cindy. And
occasionally they'd squabble over business taxes—Cindy
was emphatic about paying the quarterly estimates on
time, and Scott thought it was OK to hold off if he had a
major expense—like a new piece of equipment—to cover.

All in all, though, as Scott sees it, "We never really
fought that much." He looks back at a marriage that
was defined by great times and great friends more than
anything else, and so many people who knew them talk
about how much they loved partying with Scott and Cindy.
Theirs was a marriage whose ten-year mark deserved to be
celebrated on a hot beach in Aruba. So it was disturbing
that, in spite of the closeness they felt and expressed for
each other, they now skirmished with some regularity.

There were also some adjustments that engendered,
not anger, but a discomfort that was strange and sad for a
husband and wife. Sex for them had been fun and frequent.

Scott loved that they had had "fun in the bedroom, a lot of closeness in the bedroom."

Now what?

Paralysis doesn't make sex impossible. In fact, the doctors and therapists at Kessler spend a tremendous amount of time helping men and women and their spouses understand what is possible and how to re-explore their sexuality. Scott saw a movie during his time in rehab that outlined different approaches. Options for men cover the gamut from oral sex to use of Viagra, injections into the side of the penis, insertion of a medicated pellet into the urethra that relaxes the blood vessels and allows the penis to fill with blood, use of a vacuum pump, and surgical implantation of a penile prosthesis.

The point is, it's possible, and some paralyzed men with "complete" injuries can get erections and rediscover intimacy in ways that are truly satisfying. Scott's urologist, Dr. James Barada, who worked with Scott to find the methods that would work for him, tells his patients that, "The most important aspect is not so much that you have an erection, but that you work on the relationship in which you use it." Dr. Barada's sexual counseling focuses on the fact that, "it's not the penis, not the vagina, it's the relationship that goes into the sex that makes it a beautiful thing for intimacy."

In terms of the mechanics of sex, though, the challenge for a man is not just achieving erection but finding a way to sustain it. As Kessler's Dr. Benevento explains, facing that challenge requires exploration and patience, but it *can* be stimulating and enjoyable again, and, she says, wherever people have sensation—for Scott it was from roughly the waist up, for a quadriplegic it may be from the shoulders up or just the head and neck—those areas become more sensitive. "People can become aroused just from touching above the area of injury." In fact, Scott says that he has found himself "a lot more sensitive from my injury up than I used to be."

Of course, like Dr. Barada, Dr. Benevento reminds patients that sex and sexuality are as emotional as they are physical. "Sexuality is a lot more complicated than just the act, even for able-bodied people. A lot of the issues that occur with sexuality are more about the patient feeling that they're not satisfying the partner. For a man, if he can please his wife and she's happy, then he'll be happy, even though it's not what he used to be happy about. But if you have to use devices, it's certainly more stressful for people who didn't use those kinds of things before. And it's stressful to talk about those things, if you're not used to talking about sexual issues."

Complicating the emotions of sex for paralyzed men and women is the fear of a bowel accident, especially early on, before that whole aspect of life is mastered. "Having an accident can be even worse than not being able to perform," Dr. Benevento points out. Add to that "when the spouse becomes the caregiver," and the married relationship becomes even more challenging. It's why Dr. Benevento and her staff encourage couples to hire someone to help out with day-to-day tasks, until the patient regains independence. "Most couples would be happy to help each other through anything," she says. "But once you make that person the caregiver, it makes it much more complicated.

Think about it. You do the bowel program, and then you have to put on a negligee?"

Scott and Cindy tried. Like every other bodily function of Scott's, though, there was nothing spontaneous or carefree about it. The question was, could they find a new comfort zone, and could that new reality be as sweet? "We were young, we had to try," Scott insists, but he sensed Cindy's frustration and embarrassment. He thinks the whole idea of having to "work on it" got to her. "Maybe she didn't feel like she was being satisfied. Maybe she felt I wasn't getting pleasure out of it. I don't know." All he knew was, it was taking time and effort to figure out all the new mechanics, and, "She just wasn't that interested I don't think as before. Maybe I turned her off, I don't know." And in his frustration, he broke down one night and said to her, "I wouldn't blame you if you just left me."

"That's a hard thing to say," he says quietly. "I would have done anything to please her. I loved her so much. But I did say that. I felt that for putting her in the situation that she was in, for everything that was going on, even though it only happened by accident, I felt bad. I told her I wouldn't blame her if she left."

Outside the house, there was no sign of trouble. Everyone knew that life was tough, but just about everyone around Scott and Cindy was cheered by how they seemed to be coping, and loved seeing them enjoying the relief of friends and family, picnics and ATV rides in warm weather, and snowmobile outings in the winter. Scott was getting back to hanging out with his guys from time to time, and was hunting from his truck or at Kenny's makeshift camp in the fall.

He was just pushing the envelope more and more, like one time during the winter after his accident, when he went out with Kenny to hunt, but "we didn't exactly hunt that night," he winks. "We had a little whiskey. He says to me, 'We'll only have a little bit,' and he put his finger partway up the bottle and says, 'We won't go below this point.' Weeell, we ended up drinking a *little* more than we should've. I get back here to the house and I flip over backward in my wheelchair down in the basement. It was kinda funny actually, but that was *not* good. I laid down there for a while not feeling too good, then I called him up—it was about eleven-thirty, twelve o'clock at night— just *harassed* him. But y'know, that was fun."

Cindy was rejoining the world, too. She had her work and her family and bowling with the girls. And for both of them and their devoted organizing committee, plans for the second fundraiser, scheduled for April 7, 2001, consumed much of their free time. They were amassing prizes and gift certificates by the hundreds, visiting and writing to a wider and wider circle of businesses, sending letters and notices to media outlets, and reaching out to an expanding community of disabled individuals, inviting them to come and be a part of the event. In fact, Renee's binders of records and letters were filling with heartfelt, detailed letters from paralyzed folks all over the area, who wrote to the Remingtons to share their experiences.

Scott also took a shot and wrote to Christopher Reeve asking if he could send a video that they could play at the fundraiser to help people understand where the money was going and how it was being used. Scott was beyond words when Reeve actually complied, not with his foundation's video, but with a personal video in which Reeve spoke directly to Scott.

A letter that Renee wrote to Christopher Reeve after the second fundraiser described their reaction when the tape surprised them in the mail. "The day the video arrived, my brother Scott and I were anxious, excited and of course immediately had to view it," she wrote. "I want you to know I was filled with the most incredible joy as Scott's eyes filled with tears as you spoke to him. For the first time since his accident, I knew he felt true empathy from another person. No matter how much love and support I give to him, I can't know exactly what it's like because I'm not paralyzed, but you do. Your words were not only powerful but emotionally touching, and the irony is they have nothing to do with your being a star and everything to do with your being a caring, empathetic person! My sincere thanks for your unforgettable gift to my brother. I truly believe this world is a better place because you are in it."

As the event approached, though, Scott and Renee noticed that Cindy was less involved, less enthusiastic. But who could blame her? She had both hands more than full. She was also going out more, but who could blame her for wanting more space? There were some other things that made Scott uneasy, but he chalked them up to the overall, preternatural feel of life these days. On bowling nights, Cindy had usually ridden to the lanes with Wendy Meade, but now she seemed to be leaving earlier, going on her own, and meeting Wendy there. Cindy was also emotional at home, crying for no apparent reason, mainly at night when she and Scott went to bed. She attended the fundraiser, of course, but several friends and family members distinctly remember that she seemed distracted somehow, not into it the way she had been the year before.

It was a perfect illustration of the manic nature of their lives that, in the midst of their private upheaval, the event turned into a second annual day of magic. Once again, Scott was all nerves, anguishing over everything and worrying about whether people would show. They showed and stayed and ate and gave.

Rick Davidson remembers how crazed Scott had been when Rick first arrived with several donated kegs of Davidson Brothers beer. "He didn't even know for sure what was going to happen." But when Rick saw what went on that day and late into the night, he realized that something happened that went way beyond money, and he rightly predicted that that something would ensure an ongoing success. "I don't think they knew what they had," he says of Scott, Cindy, Renee, and everyone else who had a hand in pulling it off. "Don't get me wrong, people around here love to donate to charity, and if you can give to charity while you have a chance to win something, that's even better. But what they did here was even smarter than that. What happened was they built an immediately recognizable event that gave the community a chance to get together. So the community came out and supported it because this is a small world, they knew Scott, they knew the family, everybody was connected somehow. They gave people a chance to meet and hang out with their neighbors, where they can put in a few dollars for a chance to win a chainsaw or a vehicle or a gift certificate, drink a beer, and have home-cooked food. This is just what communities want."

Rick got caught up in it, too. "That year, I couldn't leave! I set up the beer and got it all going, and I was gonna leave, but one thing led to another! I don't even know that many of those people up there, but I ended up having such a good time, I needed a ride home!"

And, as Renee continued in her letter to Christopher Reeve, everyone who attended the event was in shock that Scott & Co. had actually landed a video straight from C. Reeve himself.

"Your video was a smash at the benefit," Renee reported. "Complete silence overtook a room packed with 500 plus people as you spoke and tears flowed freely. As the video ended, the most empowering applause and cheers filled the room. The glow on Scott's face made our day. It is so true what you said, 'Life holds so much more than any of us can imagine.' As we wrap everything up for our 2nd Annual Spinal Cord Research Benefit we are proud to say we were able to raise $25,578.00 for your foundation… Our faith is strong, a cure will be found! Until next year, my deepest thanks."

Life did hold so much more than Scott could ever have imagined when, soon after the fundraiser, Cindy broke the news to him that she had "met this guy." Scott was at a loss for what to say at first. The only thing he could think was to tell her that it was OK, in fact maybe it was a good thing if she had someone to talk to. Later, though, he pressed her about it, and she dismissed it as "nothing." He continued to try over the next week or two to talk to her about it and about everything that was happening to them, but she didn't want to talk.

Clearly, though, it wasn't nothing. There were apparently so many thoughts and feelings swirling inside her, but she couldn't or wouldn't talk them out—not to Scott anyway, or to Renee or Wendy or any of the people who had been such a big part of her married life. She started sleeping upstairs in the loft that had been their before-bedroom, telling Scott that she just needed rest.

Finally, she came home from work one evening, and Scott just sensed something was up. It's so weird to him that he has to struggle to recreate the details of that evening. "You'd think I'd be able to remember," he says working it over in his mind. He can't recall exactly what time it was or what made him think that things weren't right, but he does remember the point at which Cindy was on the couch and he was in the wheelchair, and they were talking about nothing in particular, and she said it. "This guy," she told him, "he stole my heart."

Scott tried to talk to her, but what in the world could he say, what *should* he say? He thinks he suggested that maybe she should just not see the guy anymore, but he's not sure. He tried not to panic. He was still convinced that she was struggling, as he surely was, with everything that was happening to them, but the reality was, her admission leveled him. As he conjures up the feelings of that time, the words rush out of him in a runaway train of thought.

"You're sitting in the goddamn wheelchair and you know sex ain't what it used to be, what the hell can you do to keep your woman? You're a man and you feel kinda worthless. I always loved my wife, and I loved her even more when she helped me through everything—all that stuff—and I was completely broken when she said, 'Somebody else stole my heart.' What do you have to say? And y'know, you look at yourself the way you are, and you say, 'Jesus!' It's painful. But when somebody helps you in your darkest and worst moments and then all of a sudden… boom. It's a real heartbreak there. It's the feeling like, what are you gonna do? You're paralyzed. Your woman found another man, your sexual life you're still trying to figure that out, because I didn't know, maybe I was gonna have to have a damn pump implant. I would have done anything I had to do. I really didn't want to have an operation down there, but what are you gonna do? Between all of that and all the work she was doing around here, it probably was overwhelming for her. And when you just didn't *feel* good, and you get grumpy—I know I was grumpy at times. I think maybe I was selfish at times, I'm not afraid to admit it. I'm not saying I wasn't. But still, it just hurt."

In his search for help, one of the people Scott turned to was his urologist, Dr. Barada. "I knew I was losing my wife, and I'm wondering if this [sex] is part of the problem, and I'm telling myself I gotta do something, and you're embarrassed about it, but what do you do? She's a young woman and I'm not that old, and you just can't go without having sex. So I called him up. Shoot, I was probably just about crying. I don't know if that was solely the problem…" He pauses before continuing, "I'm sure it was a lot of things, but me and the doctor kept working on it."

With guidance from his doctor, Scott did try a lot of things. He gave Viagra another try, which didn't work so well. Then injections, and that didn't work either. "Then we upped the injections *and* I popped a couple of Viagra," he says, "and that seemed to work."

But the reality was that the relationship didn't seem to be working. Nothing *felt* right.

As April 2001 approached, Scott was looking forward to the family's annual trip to Myrtle Beach. Maybe some time away in the sun would pull the plug on the tension that was building at home. As the family made plans, though, Cindy announced that she really didn't want to go. She told Scott to go ahead with the kids. Scott agreed. Maybe it was for the best—decompression time for everyone.

About a week before the family took off, Renee was over at the house visiting, and, at one point, she went out for a drive with Cindy. "We were very close," says Renee, who felt she understood as well as anyone the weight of Scott's trauma. But unlike Cindy, Renee emoted easily. She talked and cried about it on a regular basis. "Cindy and I spent so much time together, so we just went for a drive, and I said, 'Cindy, just get some counseling.'"

Cindy looked back at her and said, "No, Renee, you'll never understand." That moment left Renee with a sinking feeling that she never let on to anyone.

Unfortunately, she didn't have to. Within days of departure, Cindy admitted that she was thinking of getting her own apartment. Scott begged her not to go. "I felt so bad. I didn't want to trap her, but I couldn't stand the thought of losing her. And I honestly never thought that she'd really go."

Their personal bank account was low at the time, so Scott, wanting Cindy to feel more free and independent, wrote her a check for $2,000 from his business account. "I wanted her to feel free to go, but still I begged her not to. I told her I hoped she would be there when I got home. I knew this was serious, but I never thought she'd move. Maybe I should've stayed, not gone on the trip. I still feel bad that I went, to this day, but she also needed room, and the kids were looking forward to it. I don't know. Did I make a mistake to go? I just don't know."

The day before the family left, Renee went back to the house while Cindy was at work, and she and Scott cleaned the place from top to bottom. "I mopped every floor, changed the sheets—everything—so the whole week, she wouldn't have to do housework, she'd only have to be home alone," says Renee, who was hoping that she had read the tea leaves all wrong. "I was thinking I was doing her a favor, I was basically saying, I know this is rough, but here, now you have a week to yourself."

It was a Friday in April when the caravan—Scott and the kids; Gert and Bull; Steph, Keith, and their kids; Renee, John, and Joss; and Renee's dear high school friend, Karen, and her husband and kids—headed off on the long drive to Myrtle Beach for a week in the sun.

Throughout the weekend and into Monday, the time was uneventful, just warm and relaxing. Tuesday night, the whole crew returned from a dinner to celebrate Joss' thirteenth birthday. Gert was tired, so she and Bull went upstairs to their place, and everyone else piled into Renee and John's condo. They were all hanging out and talking when the phone rang. It was Cindy. Scott got on the phone, but it was hard to hear, so he told her to hold on a minute while he moved to the bedroom. He had been in there only a few minutes, when he hollered out, "Come here, Renee!" She went in, and with one look at the tears on his face she shut the door and said, "Scott, what's the matter?" Under the protective cover of long-distance, Cindy had told him, "I won't be here when you get home."

13.
Like the tree that hit him

Like the tree that hit him, Scott never saw it coming. Like that blow nearly two years before, he could barely breathe from the impact. Sure, the signs are all there for him now. Consciously or unconsciously, little by little, physically and emotionally, Cindy had surely been detaching from him over a period of time. How did he not suspect that it might lead to this? But he didn't, not in a million years.

After Scott broke the news to Renee, she told him, "All right, let me tell everyone you don't feel good." She walked back out to the crowded living room. "Guys, I'm sorry, but Scott doesn't feel good," she lied. "Could everybody go to somebody else's condo? He's not feeling well after dinner, something's hit him." The party moved to Gert and Bull's place upstairs. Renee suggested that Joss go, too, and hang out with Karen's daughter, Kara.

John and Renee went back into the bedroom to console Scott. Renee pressed him, "What exactly did she say? What did she mean?"

"She's not gonna be there when I get back," he told them. "She's already started to move out."

Renee's mind, as usual, went to work. "All right, let's regroup. We'll figure this out. What do you want to do?"

Scott didn't hesitate. "I've gotta go home." He was adamant. Renee tried gently to talk him out of it. She honestly didn't think that leaving was the best thing. It was only Tuesday. Maybe he should think about it a few more days, and the kids still had most of their vacation ahead of them. But staying was out of the question. He thought he could convince Cindy to stay, maybe he could fix things.

Renee realized she wasn't going to change his mind, but she persuaded him at least to wait until morning. It was already eight or nine o'clock. "We have to tell Mom and Dad," she told him. Scott knew she was right, but he was at a loss.

"What do I tell them?" he said, searching for guidance.

Renee said simply, "Just tell them the truth." Then, she picked up the phone and called upstairs. "Could you and Dad come down?" she asked her mom. "Scott wants to talk to you. Leave the kids up there with Steph and Keith."

Gert and Bull came down. Renee and John left Scott alone with his mom and dad, and went to the condo where Karen and Bill were staying to let them know what was happening. Since Cindy had called, and now Gert and Bull were needed downstairs, Steph and Keith were sure something was up. John Roscoe was suspicious, too, and surprised his aunt Steph when he told her, "I think we'll probably have to get up early and go home."

Steph and Keith took John and Jenna down to the beach for a walk before bed to give them something to do. When they got back, they put the kids to bed, and spoke to Renee. Steph was shocked. She swears she wasn't even aware that Scott and Cindy were having problems.

Gert and Bull walked into Renee's bedroom. Scott was sitting on the bed. He looked up at his mom and said, "Can you be ready to go home early in the morning?"

She said, "Yes, Scott, what's the matter?"

"Cindy just left. She moved out to Warrensburg. I want to leave as soon as I can and get as close to home as I can before the kids start asking questions."

Gert was speechless. Bull didn't know what to say. They didn't press their son for information, they just got busy packing Gert's bags.

Renee and John were up until about midnight helping to pack Scott's and the kids' things. For the most part, there wasn't much talking; everyone just kept busy. But they did have to make one decision—how Gert was going to get herself in and out of Scott's truck, a Dodge Ram 1500. It was murder for her: "I could *not* climb into his truck, no matter how hard I tried. It's so high, and my legs are so short, and I've had both knees replaced."

Someone had a brainstorm. Steph and Keith made a run to a twenty-four-hour Wal-Mart to grab a stool. They tied a string to it, so Gert could lower it down to the ground to get out and haul it back into cab of the truck once she was in.

Renee and John woke with Scott at 4:00 a.m., when he got up to shower, and finished loading his truck with his "equipment." Along with all his clothes, he had contraptions for toileting and showering, his standing chair, and the two wheelchairs that he'd brought in case one broke down.

Around 5:00, they led the kids into the truck. Jenna kept saying over and over, "Why are we going? Why are we going?" Everyone had sworn that they wouldn't say anything—Scott had demanded that he didn't want the children to know yet. Gert just said, "Don't ask any questions. We'll tell you later in the car."

Watching that truck pull out of the condo parking lot was one of the hardest things Renee has ever done. She had agonized over whether she should have been the one to go with them, but Scott had insisted that she not ruin her vacation and Joss' birthday.

"I just wanted them to get home safe. I was scared to death," she says, remembering clearly the emotions of that morning. Nine hundred miles of highway lay ahead of them, and Renee kept telling Scott, almost scolding him, 'Whatever you do, you've got to be careful! You're not in the right mindset." She worried, too, about Gert driving in traffic, driving that distance, driving in her own state of worry. "It was the hardest thing when they pulled out. My husband and I stood there in that parking lot and just wept uncontrollably. I just couldn't stop, I mean really hard cries."

As soon as Renee could compose herself, she knew whom she needed to reach. She dialed Chris Johnson. "Scott's on his way home," she told his dearest friend. "Cindy left. Please, I'm not going to be there."

"Don't worry, Renee," Chris told her. "I'll be there every single day for him until you get back."

Chris was not as surprised as he might have been. On the one hand, he honestly wasn't aware of a problem between Cindy and Scott. "From all the time I spent with them, I didn't see it," he swears. "We went to Canada, we had a great time. No sign of any problem. And this was, what, not so long after that?" On the other hand, he says, "While Scott was away, I met her on the road a couple of times, and she had a load of different stuff in the car, and I had the feeling something was up. And I tried talking to her during that time, and she didn't want to talk."

For Scott, Gert, John, and Jenna, it was the ride from hell. A surreal, eerily quiet, tension-packed affair. Gert drove only about three hours, four hours tops, of the trip. She took over only when Scott finally told her, "Mom, I've got to get off my butt for a while." He made that concession reluctantly knowing the danger of starting a pressure sore from such relentless sitting. Behind the wheel or in the passenger seat, Scott was possessed. "We drove like a hundred miles an hour," Gert recalls, shaking her head. "We drove way too fast. He was just so upset." Scott refused to waste a minute to eat, so he'd agree only to race through drive-thru windows. The only other times he stopped were for gas and bathrooms. Gert would run the kids into the rest stops, with Scott urging "Hurry up, hurry up!" And the damn stool made him crazy. "The cord on the stool was terribly thin," Gert explains. "When I got the stool down, it would twirl around, and I couldn't get it to stand flat. Scott got so impatient with me. And oh my goodness, I'm on a diuretic, I've been taking them for years, and when they kick in, you've gotta go, there's no waiting.

He wanted me to hurry up getting in and out of that truck, and I could *not* do it." As for Scott, he was not about to waste time getting *himself* in and out of public restrooms. When his own bladder was full, he pulled way over on the periphery of a rest stop parking lot and catheterized from the cab of the truck.

For nearly the entire ride, the car was dead quiet. Obviously, the kids knew that something was wrong, because they, too, barely spoke. Gert doesn't remember them ever asking or ever being told what was going on.

Gert relieved Scott behind the wheel only a couple of times. Once was when they were passing through Washington, D. C., and poor Gert was exhausted. "I was falling asleep. I could barely keep my eyes open, and all of a sudden I heard Scott holler at me, "Mother! What do you think you're doing?!' Gert was nodding out and heading straight for a concrete barrier. "If he had not hollered at me I probably would have hit it. I was so tired and I was fighting sleep, and I knew he needed rest because he was not to sit on his butt for too long. The whole thing was awful."

As if all that weren't enough, about halfway home, buzzers on Scott's dashboard started going off. They seemed to get worse every time he slowed to go through toll booths, so he hoped to God it was some weird signal from his new EZpass transponder setting something off in the truck. Regardless, he had *no* time for this. There was no room in his life or his head for the car to be screwing up. He just pressed on. The next day, he would start up the truck and find the oil pressure down to practically nothing due to a blown intake gasket.

Even with unavoidable stops for gas, food, and bathrooms—when simply getting in and out of the truck were a pain in the neck for Scott and his mom—they were back in Brant Lake by 11:00 Wednesday night. They had covered the Atlantic coast, from South Carolina to the Adirondack Mountains, in eighteen hours, a drive that usually took about twenty-two.

Scott drove first to his mom's house, just long enough, literally, for her to climb out of the vehicle. "You can have your luggage tomorrow," he told her, impatient to get home.

Gert was in agony. "Don't you want me to go with you?" she pleaded. "I was an absolutely wreck," she says. "I was scared. I'm thinking, oh these poor kids! What are they gonna do? Everything's gonna be just hysterical. And what if Cindy takes the kids, and he's all alone there?" But Scott had enough on his plate at that moment. He tore out of Gert's driveway and up the road to his house.

When Scott and the children arrived, Cindy was there, but her things were already gone. She had rented an apartment in nearby Warrensburg. Scott tried to talk to her, but she didn't want to talk or listen. He wanted to try anything—hiring help, going to counseling separately or together or both—but she was resigned. Scott was the one who finally turned to John and Jenna and explained that their mom was moving out, and, as Gert had feared, they dissolved into tears. Cindy stayed the night, sleeping in the loft, then went to work the next day and took the children with her that night.

The house went silent.

When the tree hit Scott, something mysterious ran interference between his emotions and the event. His mind wandered into an out-of-body zone before drifting in and out of consciousness. No such luck this time.

Lying in bed that strange night with Cindy upstairs and her belongings several exits down the highway, and then when she drove away the following day, he was gripped by a panic that was beyond his control and imagination.

His feelings swung wildly between wanting Cindy to stay and wanting to grant her the freedom she was seeking. Thoughts would flood his mind. He wanted his wife back. He loved her and wanted to work things out. He was scared to death about the prospect of being alone. He grieved for John and Jenna, who had already been through so much because of him, and now... this. At the same time, he says, "I wanted to show her I cared. I wasn't gonna sit here and trap her. I wanted her back, but I didn't want to push her away more by trapping her here. I realize you have to make yourself happy, and I don't want somebody to live in misery for the rest of their life, but when you have two kids, you're really wrenching on them when you leave, aren't you? Is that selfish?"

He agonized over and replayed the events of the last year and had no idea what to do with the guilt that would wash over him in waves. "She helped me through so much. God, maybe she shouldn't've. Maybe we should've had a nurse. Maybe her helping me out like a nurse wasn't a good idea. I really shouldn't have asked her to do it.

"I always wonder how I would've handled it if it was reversed. Would I have just kept working every day? She was there for me every day, and I needed her so much. I don't know what I would've done if she hadn't been by my side, and my sister, and my whole family. You can't get better without that support. I'll tell you I had so much love for her to have her help me do what she did. I just say to myself now, I should've helped her do the laundry more. I wonder all the time, could I have done something? I should've been doing the laundry. A lot of time I didn't show it like I should've that I loved her. I got so busy, and I did work a lot and go off hunting with my friends. She was right about all that. I *am* partly responsible for her leaving—gotta be—don't I? And y'know making love and this and that wasn't the same. It was all a struggle and things weren't working out, and we really didn't get our sex life worked out, it was a disaster."

His brain just worked harder and harder and harder. He didn't know what to think, what to do. What were the answers? What would make everything go back to the way it was? He had no idea.

Scott's bewilderment would not surprise the experts. The most accurate predictor of how someone—whether the injured person or the partner—is going to do after the injury is how they did prior to the injury, says Kessler psychologist Lauren Vocaturo. Look at the coping mechanisms and conflict resolution strategies they used before their lives were thrown into chaos. Scott swears on a stack of Bibles that his marriage was a good one, a happy one. Sure, they had disagreements, but nothing out of the ordinary. If Cindy thought differently, he was completely unaware. It wasn't their style to have major heart-to-heart, state-of-the-union talks. And that's just it, says Dr. Vocaturo. Bringing a life-changing accident into the household demands intense emotional support. It is a family event, and every member of that family needs to air feelings, acknowledge pain, confusion, fear, and anger, and recognize all of the ways that life has changed. For Scott and Cindy, that airing process was not their style.

Cindy did an amazing job of being strong for Scott, but she didn't confide in Scott or in their closest friends. Before the accident, if she had been resentful of the time he spent hunting, his long work hours, the fact that their bank accounts and property were in his name, she rarely let on. And frankly, in their before-life, perhaps everything good about their marriage made those annoyances relatively minor in the scheme of things. Their after-life, however, put everything in a new light. It may be, Dr. Vocaturo speculates, that Cindy reached a point where she felt, "I can't deal with your injury when there's other stuff that's been going on all along." Don't forget, too, the doctor adds, just because you think you're going to be able to handle a situation, and you want to handle it—consider the expressions of love and commitment that Cindy wrote about in the hospital journal—doesn't mean you will be able to. "Marriage may be for better or worse," she says, "well, how worse is worse?"

Dr. Benevento echoes virtually the same observation. "Marriage is hard, period. Through thick and thin, better or worse, but this is *really* worse," especially for relatively young people. And just imagine how willing you have to be to change your *entire* lifestyle. "You have to change how much income is coming into the house, what kind of cars you drive…" If you had worries or dissatisfaction before, a trauma is just as likely to render all of them moot as it is to magnify them to entirely new proportions. Unfortunately for Scott, he couldn't even fall back on the thought that things hadn't been good to begin with. For him, they *were* good. It compounded his shock to think that, for her, they might not have been so good, and that he hadn't been aware enough, smart enough, or sensitive enough to see it.

The morning she left, Scott's emotions were out of control. He felt like he was coming apart at the seams. He called his alter ego, Chris, at work. Chris dropped everything and headed to Scott's. When Chris got there, he found his best friend in a psychic meltdown. "We gotta get you out of this house," he said.

They got into Chris' pickup and drove. "We just rode around half the day, and just took it from there," says Chris. "Who knows what we talked about, we just talked or didn't talk." When you ask Chris if he realizes how important he was to Scott that day, his simple reply says everything there is to say about friendship. "He'd do the same for me."

Scott can't remember what they talked about either, but he remembers that Chris cruised around taking him to see some job sites, especially one magnificent place that was under construction on the lake—"a beautiful, big place like the old Adirondack great camps that they used to build years ago." Scott will never be able to express how much Chris helped him that day—rescuing him from drowning—and in the days after. Chris slept at Scott's house every day until Renee got home.

Unfortunately, other days followed when Scott thought he would go under. "It just hurt like hell right after she left. It hurt to know your children might be with another guy, and he's got legs, and you're thinking, shoot, if I had my legs this wouldn't've happened. It was hard every day to get out of bed, and when she left, it was even harder. After sleeping with someone for all those years, then all you got is the pillow and the dog. I know she was going through a hard time, but it still hurt like hell."

He stopped working out with his weights, and the little trucking business that he and Cindy had been getting off the ground, he "just shut it down." He would lie in bed at night and wonder, "What the hell's going on?"

"Oh, a bunch of shit runs through your mind," he sighs, "and you end up crying a lot and hugging the pillow. I was just a nervous wreck. A lot of times I couldn't eat, couldn't sleep, and my heart wouldn't stop racing. Before, you figured no matter how bad it seems, if we just hang in there, things are gonna be all right. Now, you're thinking, *are* things gonna be all right?"

Scott's family took turns spending nights with him, in part because it was obvious how much pain he was in, and in part to ease Jenna's fears. "What if there's a fire, Aunt Renee?" she begged one day. "What will happen if we're with Mommy? Who's gonna get Daddy out?"

Gert stayed some nights. Renee, John, and Joss slept over. Earle stayed, too. "My family are all go-getters," as Earle puts it. "We all love him very, very much. And we'll do anything we can to keep him up. You can't let somebody like that sit there and think all alone."

Everyone was on alert to make sure that Scott never sat too long with just his thoughts. There was good reason to worry. A lot of times, he told his brother-in-law, John, "I should've died up there in the woods."

John reassured him time and again, "Don't say that, Goober. We love you."

So they all kept a watchful eye. "We communicate amongst us," says Gert. "If somebody knows something, they'll call somebody else, and we'd just drop in—just think of any excuse to check up on him."

Their covert intelligence-gathering led to a number of rescue missions, like one night during the fall after Cindy left. It was hunting season, Gert remembers, and one of the kids called her to say that Scott was alone and kind of down. She went up to the house. Scott was there, the house was dark, and, "Oh my heart," Gert sighs, "you just have no idea." Gert went upstairs to the main living area of the house. Scott was sitting in the dark in his wheelchair.

"Whatcha doing here, Mom?" he asked quietly when she got to the top of the stairs.

"Oh, Dad's gone," she fibbed. "So, just thought I'd come up and watch TV with you."

"I was just sitting here watching for my deer," he assured her.

She doesn't know whether he was or wasn't, but she stayed anyway, for about three hours, watching whatever was on the tube. "I just couldn't come home," she says. "I thought if I stay long enough, whatever's bothering him, even if we don't talk about it, he'll get through it."

Most days, he got through it one way or another. One day, though, everything just became way too much. The pain, the meds, the loneliness, the sickening guilt over what life was becoming for the children, the disgusting reality that so much of a day can be wasted just taking a shit, and then a tense phone conversation with Cindy, when it became clear that her move was *not* going to be a fleeting need for space. She wasn't coming back, no discussion.

Scott's life had become a prison. His wife had escaped. His children were left with visiting rights between their two worlds.

So one day, to quiet the noise in his head, he had a couple of drinks. Later, Renee would discover that it had, in fact, been literally two vodka and tonics. But given how little Scott was eating, his level of anxiety and depression, and perhaps the medications he was on, those two drinks may as well have been two dozen. Sick and disoriented, he fell over in his chair onto the floor. He managed to reach the phone and dial Renee, but dropped the receiver before she could answer and it skidded out of reach. When she answered, she could hear him in the background, "Renee," he begged, "you've got to help me!"

She got hysterical, and yelled to John and Joss, "C'mon, we have to get to Scott's!" They jumped into John's truck, but knowing that it would take twelve minutes to reach Scott from Chestertown, she dialed Wendy and Ted Meade on her cell.

"Wendy!" she cried in a panic, "Get to Scott's. Something's wrong. Do whatever you have to do to get into that house!"

Ted and Wendy raced up the road, then up the outside steps onto the second-story deck. They looked in through the sliding glass doors and saw Scott on the floor. The doors were locked, so they yelled to him through the glass, but he didn't answer, didn't move. "We were hollering. We were frantic," Wendy recalls. So Ted went around the deck to the side of the house and kicked down the side door, taking the wood frame with him. They raced to Scott, and he just cried uncontrollably.

Renee, John, and Joss got there as Ted and Wendy were getting into the house. This time, Renee's response was fury—raw anger that she was losing her brother. "I was screaming at him, 'What did you take?! Tell me! What did you take?!' He was white as a ghost. He was vomiting. I was so scared. And I said, 'Scott, don't you do this to me! You made it through. You didn't die.' I started shaking him and being so angry." She was shouting and crying, and then pleading with him to get a grip. "It's not worth it," she implored. "You have two kids. You have got to find a way to go on."

Everyone on the scene that day shudders to revisit it. They also agree that it was Scott's rock bottom. "That was the biggest breakdown I saw him have," says Wendy. "He has not scared us like that again."

"Nope, never again," Renee concurs. "I guarantee that was the bottom."

Not the end of sadness, mind you. There would be more down times than Scott could ever count. As Wendy noted nearly three years later, "There's still a tear a day." But it *was* the end of hopelessness. He had no idea how he would find a way to go on. He had no clue what his life was supposed to look like now, or what his place should be in the world. But he started to reach out for answers in ways that he and no one who knew him would have imagined.

Part III.

I recently switched generations. Six months ago I belonged to Generation X, the twenty-somethings who the media claim overindulge in technology and underindulge in ambition, a generation not interested in social progress. Since becoming quadriplegic, I have entered a new generation, a generation of hope. This "Generation H" consists of people with spinal cord injuries who, for the first time in history, can reasonably hope for a cure in their lifetime thanks to recent breakthroughs in neuroscience. Generation H has a very different legacy from that of Generation X, one that can help spur progress toward a cure by generating increased funding and awareness....

The effect of all of us spreading our stories, whether we have a spinal cord injury or know someone who does, can be tremendous. Robert F. Kennedy once said, "Every time a man stands up against injustice or acts to improve the lot of others, he sends out a tiny ripple of hope. Coming together from one million different centers of energy and daring, these ripples can topple the mightiest walls of oppression and resistance." As members of Generation H, we cannot stand up, but we can let our stories stand out to topple any walls separating us from a cure.

From the article, "Generation H," by David Carmel, whose family owns a vacation home on Brant Lake. David sustained a complete, burst fracture at the C6 level in a 1999 diving accident at the age of 26.

14.
Change of heart (and mind)

Within weeks of Cindy leaving, Scott made a most uncharacteristic move. He called the Center for Independent Living at Glen Falls Hospital to ask about support groups.

"I just needed something. I had gone down to see a shrink. I was having these damn panic attacks. I felt like I was being overwhelmed sometimes by all of this, so I went and talked to this guy, a psychologist, a couple of times, but it just didn't work out. I signed the kids up to see somebody, too, because they were having a tough time, but, for me, I didn't feel like it helped. I might as well have been talking to the wall. I just didn't feel like he had any idea what my life felt like. But at first, I thought maybe this would help. I just called down there and said I wanted to get into something."

Scott drove down for his first group session, and as he was getting out of his truck, a slim, pretty woman with long blond hair wheeled up to him in the parking lot. It was

Trish, who had introduced herself at the first fundraiser. She was headed into the same session. They started chatting and the rapport was instantaneous, as if they had known each other for ages. They sat in the parking lot for who knows how long, wheelchair to wheelchair.

Scott's emotions were close to the surface back then, and no one understood like Trish. On a winter day in 1985, she had lost control of her car when it hit black ice, and she was paralyzed below the waist at the age of twenty-eight. Six years later, she and her husband divorced. "In my case, the accident just brought things to the fore that needed to be taken care of," she explains about her marriage. "When something like this happens, everything comes right to the surface." At first, the breakup was "absolutely horrible." But Trish, who was engaged at the time she met Scott and later married her fiancé, Eric Weber, ultimately came to see that, "It was definitely supposed to be the way it is. It's so much better for me the way it is now."

It was also clear to Trish during their conversation and in the next few group sessions that Scott was bitter about his life and "needed to reach out and be with other people." She was also impressed that Renee and John came to a meeting, and she was moved by their feelings for Scott. When Renee addressed the group, "she got tears in her eyes," Trish remembers. "She definitely expressed that she wished this had happened to her and not him. That's how feeling she is for him. I thought at the time, she is really going through this, too. She was just so much trying to help him."

With only a handful of members, the support group didn't hold together for long, but Scott's friendship with Trish has been powerful and enduring. They became a support group of two, and their points of connection ran wide and deep. As the middle child of nine children, Trish knew exactly what it felt like to be injured and then enveloped by a close-knit family. Sometimes it may be too much, but by and large, she sees it as the lifeline that it was. "I think the family handled him a lot like my family handled me. I can relate a lot to that. With my thing, I was supported. I was just held up through my whole ordeal."

But their most powerful connection by far has been those wheelchairs. For Scott, it was an indescribable relief to talk to her. The feeling is mutual. "I really love talking to him," says Trish. "He's at ease with me, and I'm at ease with him. And we just chitchat. It feels so good that we have this friendship, because now I feel that we're just going to be able to go far with the healing process. I feel that I have this person that I can really rely on to not give up on walking."

Trish's husband, Eric, is a caring, affectionate man, devoted to his wife. They are true companions, and Eric, who is a National Guardsman and avid outdoorsman, takes Trish hiking with him whenever he can find a trail that can accommodate her chair. Still, she says simply, there's just something about talking to someone in a wheelchair. "[Scott and I] are very different, but boy, we have something in common, and he really feels familiar to me. Our friendship has been great. I think it will only get better."

The two of them would get together regularly and talk and talk. "She knows," he says. "She knows it takes so much energy thinking about the kind of obstacles you gotta get over every day. I talk to Trish about anything."

After years of practicing medicine, Dr. Benevento was surprised one day by something that one of her patients said. This young woman, who was rendered quadriplegic in a car accident, told her, "Sometimes I want people to say, 'I don't have any idea what you feel!'" It was an epiphany for the doctor, who always tried to be optimistic and "so excited about everything that [my patients] could do." But the comment made her realize that, "It's great to be upbeat, but it's not good enough sometimes. Now I realize that, instead of just being the cheerleader, sometimes you have to look at them and say, 'Y'know what? You're right, this stinks, but here are your options.' We [able-bodied people] say all the time, 'I can only imagine how you feel.' Well, no, we can't! We can never imagine what it's like to have all of this going on."

That was the difference that Trish made. She got it.

When Scott and Trish say to each other, "I know how you feel," they really do know what it's like to be out with friends, excuse yourself to go cath in a public restroom, and then have trouble getting the catheter in right, and it's taking a long time, and you know that people are out there waiting. They nod knowingly and talk in insider jargon about the finer points of wheelchair braking systems and tire tread, like longtime co-workers at an office function.

They both have the same sense that, when most able-bodied people look at them, there's probably an assumption that paralysis is like having two broken legs, and, if you're a quad, like having broken arms, too. Most folks have no idea of the systemic implications of the condition. They both know that part of you is proud to keep all those implications invisible to the outside world, but another part of you yearns to shout, "This is hard every day!"

Scott and Trish both understand, yet struggle with, that fine line between pity and helpfulness. "You don't want people to feel sorry for you," Scott tries to explain. "You can't stand being pitied. But sometimes you just want them to understand that you're not just *sitting* in a wheelchair. It's hard. It really is a fine line. I don't know, you still want your independence. You always want that. But sometimes you do need a little help.

"I was at the grocery store last night, a guy comes up to me in the parking lot, and says, 'You need help getting in the car?' I said, 'Nah.' He goes to his car and starts it up, but he came back, and said, 'Hey, let me help you with that chair.' I had the Jeep. He lifted the chair up to me so I could just swing it into the back. Y'know, I hate to be a bother on anybody, so I just usually say, 'Nah.' But he just came over, and that was nice."

Scott and Trish know all about those fine lines. They know how much time you automatically build into every errand just for getting in and out of the car. Getting from car to wheelchair and back again—they both have the choreography down cold, reaching one arm behind to the back seat, grabbing the chair, swinging it out the driver's door, reaching back again for one wheel and then the other, leaning out of the car to turn the chair onto its side and snapping one wheel into place, then doing the other side, righting the whole thing, and then swinging their bodies out of the driver's seat onto the perfectly assembled contraption. Then, after they've gone to the store, they reverse the choreography like skilled magicians. To the outsider, it is a smooth routine. Trish and Scott know, without having to say it, the trial-error-trial-error-trial-error-trial that went into making it look easy.

Scott had sensed even before he left Kessler that Cindy should be "talking to someone." What she really needed was, not "someone," but a Trish of her own. Maybe nothing could have changed the outcome of their marriage. Perhaps the accident had simply magnified too many issues for her. Maybe their new life set them off on a journey that Cindy simply didn't want to make, under any circumstances. But Scott can't help wondering what the impact might have been if she had had a caregiver-Trish who *got it*.

Scott has loved the women in his life—his wife, his mom, three sisters, and a ton of friends—but this connection to Trish has been on a different level. They have the deep, emotional, platonic connection that girlfriends are famous for. Scott has shared deeply with his family and friends, but could the Scott before May 25, 1999 ever have imagined such an intense friendship with a woman?

He contemplates the question, and admits, "probably not." Then, thinking for a second, he realizes, "Y'know, it's really easy to talk to women. Yeah, I think so. It's comfortable. I don't know, maybe they fill a gap. I guess there's been an evolution in me."

He has thought a lot about that evolution and about everything that must have been swirling around in Cindy's head. "If she had only stuck around a little longer," he wonders. "I'm doing all those embarrassing things she used to have to help me with. I'm taking care of the house, and, yeah, I have different ideas about things. Maybe I became the guy she wanted all along."

To big sister Denise, whose family nickname is Lou, the evolution is real and dramatic. "Since he's gotten hurt, he shows his emotions, he shows his feelings. He breaks down in front of us. He's not afraid to say, 'I love you, Lou.' Y'know, it's changed him. My family's always been close, but it's brought us closer. Him and Renee were always close, but now he stops over all the time, just to visit or when he's picking up the kids—Cindy now lives a couple doors down from me. He says real easy, 'I love you, Lou,' and gives me a hug and a kiss, whereas that wasn't Scott before. It humbles you. I believe it does."

Friend Jill Wilson sees it, too. "I've seen a lot of change in Scott. I think now he's a lot more affectionate and a lot more sensitive. He's very affectionate, and he takes the time to make sure everybody knows how important they are to him now."

The evolution shows itself in his male relationships, too. In fact, an evolution is evident in both Scott *and* his friends. Virtually all of his longtime friends have been humbled by Scott's experience, blown away by his efforts to deal with it, and haunted by the specter of how they might fare in the same situation. They have responded with unabashed affection and respect.

Family friend Bill Lajeunesse, whose daughter Karen was with Renee and the family in Myrtle Beach when Cindy called, began stopping by to see Scott after Cindy left. Sometimes, when Scott was down in the dumps, he says, "I took a ride with him and just shot the breeze. Seemed to help. He's a hell of a guy, and I just wanted to pep him up. He comes to our camp sometimes, and we sit around, sometimes get in his ATV, take it up into the woods and go fishing. He's a friend, and when you're a friend, you're a friend forever."

For Chris Johnson, who had always loved Scott anyway, the impact went beyond Scott's physical and emotional trials. "This whole thing really opened my eyes. I guess I never really thought about [handicaps] before. I never thought twice about pulling into a handicapped parking spot and running into the store quick. But now I notice I do. And I get annoyed when I see people doing it. That's definitely changed."

Bull changed, too. Scott's dad is not a man of letters. He's a physical guy, a woodsman, a father who taught and loved his children by deed and example. He stayed by Scott's side in the hospital and broke down to see his boy suffering, but those feelings were never expressed in the journal that the rest of the family used as an emotional outlet and a record for Scott. That's why Scott was floored when, at a family dinner at Jimbo's to mark the second anniversary of the accident, Bull, of all people, handed him a card. "Oh man, that was amazing," says Scott. "He never writes or anything like that." That glossy card that you'd buy in a store was just so out of character, and is now one of Scott's most cherished possessions. Inside were a few dollars and a handwritten message:

Scott

I'm proud to see how far you have come since your accident I'm proud to see your doing things and not setting around feeling sorry for yourself it is good to see you with a smile on your face I love you and am very proud to have you as my son love dad

here is a little something take the kids for an ice cream or something

Scott's evolution also led him to some new and renewed male friendships, one of which was with Bill Strauss, whom he'd met in the ninth grade. In high school, Scott's game was soccer and Bill's was ice hockey, but they hit it off and hung out quite a bit together. After high school, they went their separate ways. Scott went into the woods, and Bill spent a year at Adirondack Community College, then transferred to the Culinary Institute of America. Over the next eight years, Bill got married, had a couple of kids, and worked as a chef in the New York-New Jersey area, before moving back to Brant Lake.

Scott and Bill saw each other around town and would say hello. Then, when Bill was thirty-three, his life, like Scott's, took some nasty turns. He suffered a heart attack, his marriage fell apart, and his mother became terminally ill, and Bill ended up taking care of his mom for almost a year before she passed away. When Scott came home from rehab and started getting back into the world, he began actively reaching out to Bill. "He kept saying, 'Let's get together,'" says Bill. "I'd say, 'Sure, I'd love to, but I have to take care of my mom.' That was a 24/7 job. And I was going through a difficult divorce, and I just felt alienated from friends and family. When you go through challenging times, it's easy to lose touch with people." After his mom passed away, though, Bill decided to "start living life again," and, as a big part of that, he and Scott "became good friends again."

In some ways, it was like old times. In many more ways, the two old friends connected on a new level. They got together frequently and just talked things through. Sometimes Bill would go over to Scott's house at night and cook an incredible meal, and they would hang out over a bottle of wine. Bill found Scott to be the same warm, funny, energetic guy he knew when they were fourteen. "I think if you respect people, you get respected," he says. "Scott respects people, and he's very caring, he's very honest, and he'd be willing to give anyone a hand, even if he didn't know them."

Bill also found it easy to open up with Scott, and Scott felt free to unload on Bill. In spite of Scott's iron determination to rebuild his life and his happy, confident exterior, "I think now he feels like he's not on the same level as other people," says Bill. "He doesn't feel like he's equal, I think sometimes, and I tell him that's totally not true. He's made reference to that. He's said, who would be interested in him? Women, I mean. I said, 'Scott, there's no difference between you and me or anyone else. You are who you are, and people who have any respect for themselves or anyone else look past it. There's no difference between you and me. It's just that you had an unfortunate accident, but you're still the same person I knew twenty years ago.' Scott's the same guy he always was, but, y'know, you have a life-threatening situation, you look at life different. I told him that and he's told me that, and it's true."

If Scott was discovering that he had a gentler side, and even bringing out the caring sides of many of the people around him, by the fall of 2001 he was also re-awakening his inner wildman. And on one excursion with his friend, Kenny Higgins, in particular, he got a chance to take the wildman on a test drive.

Kenny knew how much Scott missed being deep in the woods, so they piled into Scott's mule—an open, four-wheel drive ATV with roll bars extending from front to back—that had been rigged with hand controls. "I decided to take him up on this mountain where I could take him more up into the woods," says Kenny. With Scott behind the wheel, they got up there and then pointed the mule down a slight hill and edged toward a ledge, where they parked to get a great view of the valley below. With the downward pitch of the vehicle, though, Scott had to reach up to the roll bar and brace himself to keep from slipping forward. Kenny saw immediately that that wouldn't work. "You can't sit like that for forty-five minutes," he told Scott.

"Yeah, I can," Scott insisted.

"No way," Kenny said. "I can't leave you like that."

Kenny told Scott to back up the mule, only it wouldn't budge. The ground was slippery with about an inch and a half of snow, and the tires kept slipping or lodging on a log that was lying on the ground behind them. They were stuck—couldn't go forward because of the ledge and couldn't back up. Kenny's thinking, *Shit, I'm gonna have to climb down this mountain and get help*—not a good prospect with Scott left up there in the cold.

"I got an idea," Scott said. "Let me get out of here!"

Kenny shot back, "No way, how are we gonna get you back in?"

"We can *do* this!" Scott was insistent, and hauled himself out of the vehicle onto the ground. The two men, grunting and laughing, spent about the next hour and a half with Scott on the ground goosing the gas a little with one hand and trying not to get himself run over, while Kenny leaned against the front of the vehicle trying to push it up the incline. They'd move a little, then Scott would set the parking brake, while Kenny ran around back of him, grabbed him by the collar and hauled him up the incline a couple feet so Scott could reach back inside the mule and push the gas. And all the while, Scott's laughing, yelling at Kenny, "Don't you go and have a damn heart attack!"

"He's out of the vehicle, sitting on the ground laughing!" Kenny says in disbelief. "And it *is* kinda funny, 'cause he's saying, 'Ken! You're gonna have a heart attack!' He's a remarkable person. I mean he's got a lot of guts, that kid. I wished I could be the same way as him if I was ever in that situation. But he got right out, run the gas with his hand, and I dragged him probably at least fifteen yards up that hill. Then, I don't know how we did it, but I lifted him up and, together, we got him back in that mule. And oh man, we had a ball."

Scott was reaching out and letting others—men and women—reach in. In that way, he was saving his own life and allowing himself to be saved. As Earle had once said, you can't let someone like that sit alone for too long with just his thoughts. No one did. And now, when Scott was alone for too long and felt like the walls were caving in, he'd get on the phone or ride around in his snowmobile or his mule or his truck.

After talking about it for nearly two years, he also bought himself a Jeep Wrangler in the summer of 2002, cashing in on the option that Esther had offered him.

He's crazy about that vehicle, and when he needs to get out, especially when he feels down, he hops in and just drives. "Sometimes it does cross your mind, and you think, what the heck? What are you even living for when you gotta go through all this?" he says. "Sometimes, y'know, it gets overwhelming. You're frustrated. That's it really, frustrated. Sometimes you feel like just smashing something, but you know you can't. You gotta keep your wits about yourself. It gets tough. So I go for a ride in the Jeep. I usually go see one of my friends, visit with somebody, 'cause you can't sit in this house by yourself. You'll go absolutely crazy."

"He pulls up to the house and honks," says Wendy. "When we hear someone honking, we know it's Scott, and everybody comes running. That's if you can get your shoes on fast enough!"

When he bought that Jeep, it was a proud day. "I was on a job," says his brother-in-law, Bill. "My father happened to be logging with me that day, and we see some guy in a Jeep come driving up. I looked at my father and said, 'Now who the hell is coming?' He come in to show me. He's remarkable. 'Course I won't tell him that, just 'cause he gets me in some awful ordeals! And I remember the first time he got his four-wheeler stuck. He got off the thing, got limbs under the wheels, and was mud from head to toe, but he got it out. He was tickled pink."

Scott remembers that one, too. It was summer of 2001, "I headed out to take a ride and didn't tell nobody where I was going. I headed up into the woods around here back of my house, and I was gonna come out another road down by my mother's house. Well, I got down in there and got stuck in the mud. A log got hung under the rear end of the machine. There I was, down this thing, stuck, nobody knows where I am, and it's probably 4:00 in the afternoon. Didn't have no cell phone. The bugs were terrible, and I had shorts on. So I said I better get down. I lifted myself onto the ground, started digging with my hands, started working the gas a little bit and finally got it loose. Grabbed the roll-bar and hauled myself back up into the machine, and this is probably an hour-and-a-half later. This was before that time with Kenny. At least I had somebody there when I was with him."

Scott was cooking his own food, cleaning his own house, doing his own laundry, pushing the snow off his own deck with a shovel, plowing his own driveway, dressing himself, managing his bodily functions, and buying his own groceries by navigating the supermarket aisles with one hand on a wheel of his chair and one hand on the cart: "It gets a little tough when you're buying $250 worth of groceries, then sometimes I need help getting it out to the car, but most times I manage."

"All of this stuff confirms it," says brother-in-law Bill. "He'll talk at times that he's giving up. People that give up don't do stuff like that. I mean, right down to keeping his wood fire going at his house. We come and split it, and his father puts it in his woodshed, but it still takes a lot for him to come down there every three or four hours to put it in the stove. What else do we do on two legs that he don't do in that chair?"

Scott thought about Cindy and the life he should have been living every hour of every day, but he was overcoming.

If he *were* going to lose it, though, if something *were* going to take him back to rock bottom, it might well have been his relentlessly uncooperative bladder. The process that he'd been following since Kessler of intermittent catheterization—threading a rubber tube through his penis and into his bladder every few hours—was not working. If he wasn't contracting his umpteenth UTI, he was leaking all over himself. Even when he carefully restricted his intake to a few sips of liquid before going out, he could never be sure that he'd stay dry. The time he took John and Jenna to the Operation Santa Claus fundraiser in Brant Lake was a perfect case in point. They all piled into Scott's truck for the short ride, all psyched for a great time, and, when they arrived, Scott transferred out of the cab onto his chair only to find his pants soaked through. By this point, the kids had grown remarkably tolerant and understanding, but there was still a bunch of moaning among all three of them when Scott broke the news that they had to turn around and go all the way back home, so he could change his pants.

Toward the end of 2001, he was in and out of his urologist's office for help with what doctors call his "neurogenic" (having to do with nerves or the nervous system) bladder. Depending on the patient, a neurogenic bladder doesn't fill or empty completely, because the nerves that carry messages to the brain telling the muscles to hold or release urine at the right time don't work properly.

"Paraplegics come in all varieties," explains Dr. Barada, so their issues depend on "which pathways are still active and which are completely deactivated by the injury." Scott had a "fairly complex injury, not your run of the mill spinal cord injury," not because the accident deactivated all his pathways, but because some were deactivated and some were preserved, and those that are preserved act like they have minds of their own.

"In Scott's case, he has a spastic bladder and a spastic external sphincter," says Dr. Barada. That situation led to a couple of frustrating problems. Because of the spasticity—involuntary contractions—in the bladder, "when his bladder would overfill, he would leak at fairly high pressure." Scott was also having difficulty actually getting the catheter into his bladder because of "significant external sphincter spasm… which is almost rhythmic in nature," as Dr. Barada explained in his office records.

There are fibers of muscle, called sphincters, wrapped around the urethra (the exit route for urine) that squeeze to cut off the flow of urine and release to let the urine pass. The internal sphincter works by reflex. The external sphincter is the one that able-bodied people can control, but Scott can't. Because his was frequently going into spasm, not only was it difficult to empty the bladder completely, but it also became a crapshoot as to whether he could actually get the catheter where it needed to go. The external sphincter would often clamp the urethra shut and stop the cath in its tracks.

With catheterization, says Dr. Barada, "This is not one of those things that allow you to be 90 percent. You have to be 100 percent in order to function normally." Thus, Scott was struggling to cath, leaking urine, and suffering from infections because urine, which is a terrific fertilizer for bacteria, was often left too long in the bladder.

Dr. Barada experimented with some medications to try to make the bladder and sphincter relax. None was effective enough.

As a stopgap, Dr. Barada put in a Foley catheter, a tube that extends through the penis and into the bladder and stays in place, emptying into an external bag. Some people, quadriplegics for example, have Foleys in place permanently, because they are unable to handle intermittent catheterization or don't have aides to do it for them. The Foley was not the long-term solution for Scott. "As you know," Dr. Barada points out, "he has a very vigorous lifestyle." Scott was not about to wear a permanent tube and bag. He wanted to wear shorts in the summer. After struggling to regain upper body strength, he had taught himself to swim without a flotation device. He had a wave runner and snowmobile to ride. And Scott found that the Foley made sleep even more of a drag than it had already become. "You can't lay on your stomach. You gotta lay on your back all night long, and that's one of the big drawbacks. Other people might be able to go on their side, but I can't, 'cause then my shoulders kill me."

Dr. Barada laid out the options. Scott could have a sphincterotomy in which the sphincter is cut to disable it and stop the spasms. The price of relief, according to Dr. Barada, was that, "He would be completely wet, continuously, and he'd have to wear a condom catheter in order to collect the urine." Like a traditional condom, a condom catheter is a plastic sheath that fits over the penis, but it has a tube at the end that allows urine to drain into a pouch that can be emptied into the toilet. Scott rejected that option out of hand. Incontinence was out of the question. Instead, he chose a Mitrofanoff procedure. Named for a French surgeon, it's an operation in which the doctor would fashion a new catheterizable conduit through Scott's belly button—creating a new entryway to the bladder that bypasses the sphincter and urethra altogether.

In January 2002, Scott underwent the operation. Dr. Barada took a piece of Scott's small bowel and reconfigured it to make it smaller and tapered, and connected it to his bladder. Then he created an opening through the belly button, so that Scott could pass a catheter through it, down through the tapered section of bowel and into the bladder.

The procedure went fine, and Scott was only supposed to be in the hospital about three days. Three days, though, turned into eight, when Scott developed an ileus, also known as gastrointestinal stasis, which is a delay in the recovery of bowel function. The condition is not uncommon after abdominal surgery, particularly in someone with neurogenic bowels as a result of spinal cord injury. Unfortunately, it's not a simple matter of just waiting for the excretory system to get back to work. When the colon remains inert, gas accumulates in the small bowel, and, as happened to Scott, the patient is hit with abdominal swelling, nausea, and vomiting—common symptoms of ileus.

Scott was furious when doctors had to insert a nasogastric or NG tube through his nose and throat and into his stomach to suck out the liquid and gas that was putting pressure on his gastrointestinal tract and making him sick. There's no question that the tube relieved the nausea and vomiting, but Scott had first to endure the watering eyes, gagging, and pressure in the nose and throat that make insertion a hideous memory for most patients. When the tube gets past the back of the mouth, the doctor or nurse waits to feel the patient swallow against the tube. People can't breathe and swallow at the same time, because a swallow closes the little opening at the top of the windpipe, called the glottis, shutting off access to the lungs. It's the action that protects us from inhaling what we eat and drink. The swallow offers the opportunity to push the NG tube further down into the stomach without accidentally sending it into a lung.

Scott was beside himself. "They had to stick the thing into my stomach, drain all the pressure out of my stomach. Oh, I'm telling you, I swore to God, I said I'm never coming to the hospital again. I'd rather die first. That tube down your throat. That's torture! I had it for three days, and had nothing to eat for eight days, not even a drink of water. Oh man."

He ultimately cleared that hurdle, though, and went home to enjoy his new plumbing. But within months, it was déjà vu. Once again, there were problems getting the cath in smoothly every time. The tube made it through the belly button conduit just fine, but then would not always enter the pouch created from Scott's small bowel—the one that was connected to the bladder. "If you could imagine a pipe [belly button]," Dr. Barada explains, "and at the bottom of the pipe you put in an ice cream cone upside down, so the point is inside the pipe. You push the catheter down the pipe, and, instead of going into the bottom of the ice cream cone, it bounces off to the side. It goes smoothly up to that point, but once it gets to that little cone, instead of going through the cone into the bladder, it bounces off."

Toward the end of 2002, as all of this was coming to a head, Dr. Barada gave Scott some "tricks" to try in the hopes of avoiding another surgical fix. Those tricks included injecting a liquid through the conduit and trying to cath lying down, both of which can stretch the cone and hopefully make it easier to get the catheter to slide through. Neither was the answer. Both Scott and Dr. Barada were sorely disappointed. Dr. Barada sums up their feelings perfectly: "It really bites, because we did [the surgery] in the first place so he could catheterize 100 percent of the time." It was finally decided that one more surgery was, in fact, the answer, which would allow Dr. Barada to "go down and straighten out the tube a little bit and chop off the end, and make it nice and neat."

As anxious as Scott was to get the issue resolved, he told the doctor to hold off for a few more months, just until snowmobiling season was over. Scott resigned himself to putting in a Foley catheter whenever he went snowmobiling during the winter of 2002 and into 2003, "so I don't leak all over."

As Dr. Barada puts it, the surgery was "in Scott's time," and that's fine, he says. "I take care of people. I don't take care of bladders. Scott's been a good trooper in all these things. He is a very easygoing guy. It's almost like I have to hold him down to keep him in one place long enough to do stuff, because he's exceedingly active with his kids and his lifestyle. I take care of a lot of people, and there are some that you become very close to. His personality with or without his spinal cord injury is dynamic and enjoyable. I know his injury was a logging accident, and although he's not able to do his physical labor, he hasn't let that interfere with his quality of life. He's a great dad and has a terrific outlook on life that would be nice to bottle and give to some other patients. He's one of those who—there but for the grace of God go I—but if it were to happen, boy, I hope I would come through it the way he has."

Perhaps Nick had it right that life never gives us more weight than our shoulders can bear, because Scott's pesky bladder alone might have sent him to the depths of depression, but it didn't. He had a life to get on with and, toward the end of 2001, another fundraiser to plan. His third annual was scheduled for April 27, 2002, and he was determined that each year would be bigger and more lucrative than the last. That is, until he and Ed went down to chat with Rick Davidson about helping out again with beer and publicity.

They were enjoying lunch and a few microbrews at Davidson Brothers and talking with Rick about their plans, when Rick stopped them. "Y'know," he said, "I think there may be something going on that day." He pulled out his calendar, and, sure enough, a business expo held every year at the Glens Falls Civic Center, usually around St. Patrick's Day, had been moved to April 27. The expo is a major area event that draws thousands of people and is supported by Davidson Brothers and the local radio station.

Scott and Ed were stunned. "They just sat there when I told them," says Rick, who quickly reassured them that, "There's no way that anybody who came to your event before is going to forgo it for the expo." But he could see that they were really worried.

Scott looked at Ed and then Rick, and said forlornly, "I guess we won't need that much beer."

"Oh my gosh," Rick says laughing, "they were two sad sacks sitting there. Although, that may have been a ploy to get me to buy them more beer."

As if that weren't enough, the terrorist attacks on New York City that September made a clear impact on their solicitations. As Ed made his yearly rounds, people welcomed him as usual and gave what they could, but "it was harder," Ed admits. "People had been giving so much to all the 9/11 victims and the New York firefighters and police officers."

Scott, as usual, could barely sleep leading up to the event, yet, once again, his committee and his community came through. Businesses had offered hundreds of small prizes and gift certificates for the raffle, including the grand prizes of an ArcticCat 4x4 ATV, a Sports Pal Canoe, and a bunch of camping equipment. There were seven bands, free hors d'oeuvres, and a DJ from the local radio station. The crowd, which again numbered between 500 and 600 people, partied, spent, and was nearly brought to tears when Joss-Elyse and several of her friends sang a musical tribute to Scott.

There was also the moment for Scott when forester Johnny Pratte worked his way through the crowd and reintroduced himself. Johnny's last glimpse of Scott had been on May 25, 1999, when the doors of the waiting ambulance had slammed shut. Johnny had heard about the fundraiser through the logging grapevine and decided to go, but he assumed that Scott would never remember him: "It was the first time that I'd seen him since the accident, and he was kind of out of it during that whole thing."

Johnny approached Scott, and was shocked when Scott recognized him immediately. Scott was genuinely touched that Johnny had made the effort to come, and they shared a laugh remembering what a first day on the job Johnny had had. "Aw man, bad luck!" Scott kidded him.

The total take that day in ticket sales and direct contributions to Christopher Reeve came to $24,976.48, bringing Scott's three-year donation to roughly $71,000.

The Remingtons' friend and Jimbo's manager Stacey Dobbs already figured that she had seen everything after Scott's first two fundraisers. But on the heels of 9/11, this was something else. "All I can say is that, for a town as small as Brant Lake, they have been absolutely, incredibly supportive of Scott—of one person—and it just blows me away how many people showed up. The room was packed. It makes you think that, after everything we'd all been through in the past year, there are some really, really great people out there. *Really* great people."

Scott's outlook was shifting. It was not about *accepting* his injury, the breakup of his marriage, or the obstacles that cluttered every single day. In fact, he can't stand the concept of "acceptance" as it relates to his situation. He is emphatic that soldiering on and even rediscovering happiness is not about accepting. To him, acceptance means giving in. That's not an option. "You can't give up hope. You gotta have hope. I don't want to think I'll be in this wheelchair the rest of my life. Hey, some people say you have to face that. Well, I believe that I don't have to. I think there's a chance that might not happen. And you gotta keep that little bit of hope that you won't be like this the rest of your life, because nobody wants to be like this. It's not an easy life on anybody to be in a wheelchair. I'm sure people have worse lives than I do. But there's struggle here, a lot of hard changes, a lot of heavy feelings. There's a lot of good things that have happened, I'm not saying there's not. A lot of good things have come out of this as far as the benefit, raising money, a lot of things I probably wouldn't have realized in my life. But you still want your legs back and you still want to go back to what you did before. I always want that hope."

Renee feels exactly the same. "We still cry, and, to this day, I can't look at a video that has Scott walking. None of us can. I don't think we'll ever completely accept this. Even with everything positive that's come out of this for Scott, for our family, and for our community, if you could do anything you'd do it to get your life back the way it was. We don't accept this. We still hold out hope. We always will. To this day, I think if you accept that this is the way you're going to be for the rest of your life, then you are giving up hope. I do believe things will change. I totally believe it will change. I don't know as though I'd want to get out of bed every morning if I didn't."

Given Scott's drive to help the world find a cure, and the reverence that he holds for Christopher Reeve as the standard bearer for the cause, people regularly ask Scott, do you think there will really be these advances? He jumps all over that question. "C'mon, let's get it done! I'm ready for the risk. Wouldn't bother me a bit. What the hell, am I gonna end up with bladder cancer or something? Putting the damn catheters in all the time, I could die of infection. You gotta think about sores all the time. Even if the cure wasn't perfect, if people could get on their feet and walk a little bit, that would be great. If you had your bodily functions back, that would be great."

How can you accept, he continues, that, "you're never really comfortable. Sitting in a wheelchair all day long, you're never *really* comfortable. If anyone sits too long, they want to get up and walk around. Well, I can't get up and walk around. So I gotta do something different, like sit in my easy chair or get in my standing chair if I'm home. Even though they say you can't feel your ass, you feel like you need to do *something* different. And y'know, your legs ache. I don't know if it's phantom pain or if it's real pain, I don't have any idea. And every now and then I get sharp nerve pain, like a knife going through me in the stomach area, right on the borderline of where I was hurt."

The outlook that he was developing stemmed from a roiling combination of his resolve to deal with his new life's relentless frustrations, adamant refusal to accept his status as permanent, and, at the same time, the discovery of so many new, sweet things that life has to offer—things that he never saw with such clarity in the "before." And among his most profound and life-affirming discoveries were the two kids who came bounding up his stairs every other day, filling his home with noise, and hanging all over his wheelchair like blankets.

15.

High and way inside

Scott always adored his kids, but even he admits that, *before*, his quality time with them had been limited. He coached their Little League and soccer teams, indoctrinated them in the finer art of snowmobiling, and tossed them around on Myrtle Beach. But he was the dad, the working stiff. Between the demands of his business and hunting expeditions with his friends, he was primarily the breadwinner, and Cindy was the chief nurturer.

In the *after*, where his world revolved around his home and where his emotions and worldview had shifted, he was blown away by the depth of feelings he had toward John and Jenna. His arrangement with Cindy was that the children would be with him every other night, and he couldn't stand it when they were gone.

Even when they tick him off, Scott ends every story about his kids with the refrain, "… but they're really great kids." Like when Jenna put her little foot down one afternoon after school and refused to study for a geography test no matter what, or when John got his snowmobile stuck in the woods by the house, after Scott specifically told him to stay on the path that Scott had just cleared. "John come running up to the house looking for help," Scott says, exasperated, "got his snowmobile stuck down by the old house next to my house. I broke a trail, said, 'Stay on the trail,' and, what's he do? Gets off the trail! Now he's buried down there. I told him, 'Get it outta there!' He's down there now lugging and tugging. He's gonna be *real* tired. He'll be hungry by the time he gets back up here."

Even when he's at his wits' end, Scott can barely believe how they fill up his heart. "So much of this [situation] is getting through stuff mentally," he says. "There were times when I definitely thought about suicide. You think, what are you worth to other people? But you can't do that when you got two young kids. It's hard to describe how much the kids have helped me. You focus on them and you get through. They're number one and that's the way you gotta live your life. And it doesn't matter if you're a successful businessman or somebody who went bankrupt, they don't care. You can tell it doesn't matter to them."

The way his life turned out, Scott had an opportunity to be a bigger part of his children's lives, to influence them in ways that he never realized before. But even more profound was how much two ragamuffins could influence *him*, teach him, and keep him grounded.

Even before the first fundraiser, Jenna—who was not yet eight at the time—had clearly soaked up more of what was going on than anyone suspected, when she announced that she wanted all of her birthday money to be sent to spinal cord research. And it was hard to believe that, when her third-grade teacher asked the children to write a Thanksgiving essay for the year 2000 on something they were thankful for, she came up with:

Happy Thanksgiving. I'm thankful for my dad because he is alive today. He is very lucky to have survived from a logging accident May 25, 1999. He almost died from not breathing when a tree fell on him. But my Uncle Earl noticed that my dad was not where he belonged. Uncle Earl found him and called the ambulance. They came and my dad was stuck onder a top of a birch tree. When my cousin Adrian told me that my dad was hurt I was sad. But I'm very lucky he is alive and he loves me a lot and I love him a lot too. I don't tack him for granted. By Jenna R.

Scott will tell you in a tone that mixes pride with utter disbelief that, every year since his accident, when someone has asked his children what they want for Christmas, they've said, "for Dad to walk." And he doesn't know how many times he's told them he's going to the supermarket, and they've offered to forfeit a lesson, a game, or hanging with a friend to help him out, "*and they're just little kids.*"

He can't take them deep into the best parts of the woods like his dad did with him, but Scott has taught John and Jenna to hunt, respecting the woods and their guns. Completing the legacy, he instructed them how to prepare fresh kill, easily accepting that his children are turning into two distinct individuals. "I gutted one this year," he said in November of 2002. "Jenna was right in there helping me. John Roscoe, don't know what kind of hunter he's gonna be." And with a gentle laugh, he tells you that John's "always saying, 'Ahhhh, that's gonna make me sick!'" But Scott, without judgment or pressure one way or the other, tells his boy, "C'mon, that's the way they are. As long as you don't cut into the guts, it's not too bad. If you cut into the stomach or you shoot it in the stomach, it smells a little bit. But if you don't, you just get a little blood on you, and it's actually nice if it's real cold out, 'cause it's warm."

John may recoil at deer guts, but one day when he and Jenna were sitting on the couch in Scott's living room, and Jenna shrieked at the sight of a bug crawling across the backrest, John reached right over, plucked it off the cushion, and turned it over this way and that, examining it carefully. You'd think he'd take this golden opportunity to terrorize his sister with that bug. Instead, he squeezed it between his fingers till it cracked, hopped off the couch to chuck it in the trashcan, and told her, "Don't worry, the thing's not gonna hurt ya."

And, unlike her brother, Jenna is a roller coaster addict, but John's the image of his dad when he climbs onto a snowmobile. During the relentless winter of 2002, Scott took his machine out onto the frozen-solid Brant Lake and pushed it up to 100 miles an hour. Then he let John take a try, and the son of a gun got it going just about as fast. "Whoooa!" Scott yelled to him. "Jeez, slow it down!" But Scott tells that story with a smirk that says, "That's my boy!"

That was also his boy, who, in the fall of 2002, was in the living room of Scott's house and caught sight of a buck outside. Scott told John to go get his rifle, the .30-06. John came back with the gun, but, for the first time, Scott got another idea. He turned to his son and asked, "Do you want it?"

John's eyes widened, "Yeah, can I?"

John went back to Scott's gun case and took the rifle that Scott had been teaching him to shoot, the .30-30. The boy snuck out onto the deck and crouched down below the rail. Jenna watched intently as Scott quietly rolled behind his son. Then, John impulsively jumped up to take aim, and Scott was sure his son had blown his chance. The buck got startled and ran. Scott held his silence, but he's thinking, "Oh nooo, what are you *doing?*"

John kept his eye fixed, and fired. Jenna shrieked, "Dad! He got it!" Scott rolled back into the house and called Ted Meade down the road. Ted came right up. He helped the kids gut John's deer in the woods, and the three of them dragged it up to the house, where Scott snapped a bunch of pictures of his boy kneeling beside his first kill.

"A five-pointer," says Scott, smiling from ear to ear. "Watching my son do that was better than me doing it myself. I can't explain the feeling. I just can't explain it. My boy, he's growing up."

Both John and Jenna can be fun, rambunctious blabbermouths, but in general, "John has always been the quiet one," says Grandma Gert, "not bubbly like Jenna. I think John holds back a lot of his feelings, and I wish sometimes he'd talk about them, scream about them, whatever. But he keeps it inside. Jenna always comes out with things. You do not have to ask with that one."

Scott marvels at how they're different from each other and from him. He loves them for those differences and has nothing but awe and respect for what they've been through. In his home, he imposes rules and chores and manners, but he's also been deliberate in making his house a safe haven, where they can ask him anything and be themselves. "He's shown them that he can still be their dad," says Renee, "and they're very, very protective of Scott."

As a result, they are normal, energetic kids, who have processed the trauma of their father's accident in a surprisingly mature way. They can't sit on a couch together for one minute without demonstrating the singular world of a twelve-year-old brother and ten-year-old sister—constant poking, giggling, and shoulder-bumping. The contact escalates to the point where one lunges on top of the other and they roll off the couch in a tangle onto the floor. A minute later, they're sitting again, but John is soon lying across the top of the couch, a perfect perch from which to roll down onto Jenna. He does, of course. Yet all the while, they hold a perfectly coherent, remarkably insightful conversation about their father's experience, which is also their experience.

Jenna agrees that all their friends and relatives got it right. "When it first happened I talked about it a lot. I really wanted to know more. I wanted to know what happened. I think John was really sad, but I took it more easily and he took it more hard. When me and John went to see him in the hospital, we were really scared. John didn't want to go to school the next morning."

John nods. "I think I was just scared." Then he offers that, a couple of years after his dad's accident, "A guy in Bolton, a logger like my dad, got hit by a tree and died. I think about that—my dad survived and stuff, and it's hard to believe."

Typical of women, Jenna talks easily about her feelings, and she admits that she "has dreams." In one recurring nightmare, Scott is in his wheelchair and there's a fire in his house and he can't get out. In another, "There's a murderer in the house and he chopped off my dad's legs, and my dad couldn't feel it so he couldn't tell us." In the next moment, though, she recounts how much fun it was to live with relatives and with the Wilsons when her dad was in the hospital, how great they all were to John and her, and how, "When Aunt Renee was watching us, she was always calm with us, taking it one step at a time, not telling us all at one time."

And they're just little kids.

It has become obvious to friends, the depth of the relationship that has been building among the three of them. Bill Lajeunesse gets a kick out of seeing them together. "Jenna has her own little ATV. Roscoe—that's his son's nickname—he's got his. Scott goes with them. They all go out in the woods. They help him and never complain. He'll ask them to get this and get that, and they just get up and do it. And Jenna's a funny little kid. Anytime anything breaks, she wants to get out the wrenches and stuff and help out."

Jill Wilson, too, notices that, "Toward his kids, [Scott's] a different person altogether. His kids are his life now. He's a good dad. He was a good dad then, too, but he's so much more involved. He has a real relationship with them, which is great to see, and they love him so much."

Scott's sister, Stephanie, has seen his warmth spread to all the Remington cousins. Scott has an above-ground pool, and in the summer, she says, "my kids will call him up and say, 'Uncle Scott, can we come up?' And he always says, 'Come on up!' And I always ask him, 'Are you sure you can handle them?' And he says, 'Oh, don't worry about me.' And he's got all the kids just hanging out with him without help. He just has the kids around. He even took a bunch of our kids to the movies once. And when he got there, the ramp was real steep, and he didn't know if he could get into the theater, but all the kids got together and pushed him up the hill."

And that's why, when it came time again for Little League in the spring of 2002, and he knew that, with Joss now out of the league, his brother-in-law, John, would be hanging up the spikes, maybe it was time to grit his teeth and face the crowd.

At a meeting just before the 2002 season, the Brant Lake Little League faced some tough decisions related to league contraction. The previous year, the league had had to cut a team, and fewer sign-ups meant that another team would have to go this year. Since Scott's team, the Chiefs, had been the last one brought into the league, it was the next one in line for the chopping block. But Karl Dingman, who works for the state highway department and whose son, Noah, was about to play his last Little League season, didn't think it was fair for Scott's team to be cut. "My team, the Bobcats, only had seven players," he explains. "We needed twelve and our sponsor was questionable. Scott's team had enough players, a good sponsor that had been funding them for a long time, and it just didn't make sense to me that they should eliminate Scott's team. So I said it would make more sense to drop my team." Scott turned to Karl at that meeting and invited him to help coach the Chiefs, which would make Noah an automatic member of the team. The other six Bobcats would go into a draft. "I was a little nervous coming home from that meeting," Karl says with a laugh.

He walked through the door, and his wife, Ann, asked him, "So, how was the meeting?"

"Well," Karl answered, "I lost the team!"

Karl knew Scott a bit because Brant Lake is such a small town, and Scott had coached Noah in t-ball six years before, but Karl didn't know Scott well, and he, Ann, and Noah didn't know the other Chiefs. But as far as Karl is concerned, "It worked out great. A positive experience from start to finish. It was definitely my most enjoyable season for sure, because of the help and the commitment of the other men—besides the fact that we were winning, which was a new experience!"

Scott was on his way. With Karl helping, the Chiefs had a coaching staff of three. Steve Bureau, another Brant Lake logger, had known Scott for years, because they had been in the same business, and because his son, Steve Jr., and John Roscoe are the same age and started in the league at the same time. Steve had been helping Renee's husband, John, with the Chiefs, and was back for another season to help Scott.

Karl wasn't sure what to expect. "I didn't know how much control Scott would have over the practices," he admits, "whether he'd rely on other adults." Scott's brother-in-law, John, also wanted to make sure that Scott would be OK, so he showed up for the first practice. That was the last Little League practice that John ever attended.

Scott, John Roscoe, and Jenna beat the team to practice nearly every time. Scott showed up the first day with printed schedules and organized drills, and later, he would come to every game with a printed roster. Later in the season, if a practice had to be changed, Karl always told Scott to give him half the list of kids so he could help with the phone calls. "Scott always said, 'No, I'll take care of it.' He did it all," says Karl, "and he was always so conscientious and respectful [of Steve and me]. He'd say, 'I'm thinking of having a practice tomorrow or some other day, how would that work for you?' There was no doubt, he was the head coach." Ann Dingman, who had been very involved in the league and kept the stat book at every game, saw it, too. "He took control right away from the beginning of the season. From the first practice, he had it set up—you go do this, you go do that. He definitely took charge of the head coach position."

At practices, Steve and Scott mainly worked with the more experienced players, while Karl would take the younger ones into the outfield to go over fundamentals— fielding fly balls and grounders and "knowing what you're going to do with the ball before it comes to you." For the most part, Steve handled batting practice, but Scott would often take a player aside, have him face the backstop, and Scott would toss a ball straight up, while the child hit into the backstop. Most days, by the time kids started arriving, Scott was there with a glove on, playing catch with John and Jenna, or "Occasionally," says Karl, "if he beat us to practice, he'd be right there at home plate hitting the ball. He's incredible."

Neither Karl nor Steve had a clue that Scott might have been apprehensive. "I never noticed that," says Steve, "and I always felt like the kids were at ease with him, because he has that manner about him. I really can't speak for his first year, but that year, the kids all really liked him. He's just that kind of guy."

When the games started, it was clear that the team and coaching staff had gelled. The team went ten and two during the regular season, winning the division. During games, Scott called the plays, but the coaches consulted constantly, and Scott always wanted his coaches' opinions, especially when it came to the pitchers' performance, given that John Roscoe and Karl's son, Noah, were the two starters. "Scott would always second-guess, or look at myself or Steve or Ann," says Karl, "wondering, 'Should I pull him?' Or he'd say, 'You wanna go out and talk to John, 'cause he doesn't want to listen to me?' And I'd say the same thing about Noah."

When Scott did need to talk to a pitcher and calm him down, there was no hesitation this year. He wheeled partway onto the mound or called the child to the third base line. It was his team.

It was also a season with built-in drama. "We had a really good team, and we went pretty far," says Steve. "We had close games a lot of times, and we were on pins and needles. We kept looking at each other like, we're gonna have heart attacks! What I saw was that Scott was so into it. His handicap and whatever other problems he was having just were nonexistent while he was on the Little League field. Something like that, God forbid, ever happened to me, I hope I could handle it like he did. I'm sure there's a lot of things we didn't see that he was going through, but he certainly never showed that he was having a hard time."

No team wins without talent, and the Chiefs certainly had that. But talent doesn't always make winners. Winning is the result of leadership, subtle chemistry among players and coaches, and an understanding that we're all in this together and it's our job to watch each other's back. It's interesting to speculate on the role that Scott's condition might have had on the chemistry of the Chiefs.

On the one hand, he was just a good guy and a good coach. Both Karl and Steve noticed exactly the same thing, that after a practice or two, no one really noticed the disability. "I just don't think the kids even saw it anymore," says Karl. "There was just nothing odd about it. It just didn't matter." Steve echoes that thought. "By the second practice, I wasn't even aware of his handicap. It was never thought of. He was the head coach, and you didn't realize in any way that he was limited."

On the other hand, Ann believes that, "The kids were more respectful without knowing it. On our other teams, when we had to pick up our equipment at the end of a practice or game, it was always, 'C'mon you guys, help!' But you didn't have to ask as much with Scott's team. The older kids and his son, especially, were very helpful."

It's clear that Scott went out there, like every other parent in every other Little League, to be involved with his kids. Along with two other great coaches who cared about the kids and about teaching the fundamentals, he made being a Chief a positive experience. However, while he didn't mean to, he also penetrated the collective consciousness of his Chiefs—coaches and players alike. "When the kids all run to their parents' cars, and you're left to bring the equipment bag to Scott's truck, then you realize, we don't really have any problems," says Karl. "Or

Scott will get out of his truck, and he'll start to leave, and he's just sitting there and not moving. And I'll say, 'Do you need anything, Scott?' And he says, 'I'm just trying to decide if I should grab a sweatshirt.' And it's something we take for granted, y'know? It's like, I'll just run back to my car if I need a sweatshirt. It makes you realize, I guess we really don't have any big problems in our life."

It was just as much a "growth experience" for Scott. "Little League has been great for me," he says. "It really helped me come out of my shell. Now I'll go out on the field, out on the pitcher's mound. I always wondered what the parents would think, but they've been great, so supportive. When John first said to me that I should take it over after Joss finished in the league, oh man, I didn't think I could do it. But it was just a great season, and I couldn't have done it without Steve and Karl. We were a great team."

Once you've made it through a season as the head coach of a Little League team, there probably aren't many other challenges—of a political, managerial, athletic, social, or diplomatic nature—that you can't handle. Still, few dads—*very* few dads—dare to venture into the world that Scott tackled next. The class trip.

First, there was Jenna's fourth grade trip to Lake Placid, which he managed with great success, chaperoning a small group of her classmates. Jenna loves that "All my friends would come over and say, 'Do a pop-a-wheelie, Scott!' He'd like ride around and pop a wheelie. All my friends think he's so cool, 'cause he can do stuff. He can snowmobile, he has an elevator in his house and a truck with a lift thing.

But they also just think he's cool himself. He's nice to all our friends."

Feeling flush with confidence, Scott signed up to accompany John's sixth grade to Albany. Scott followed the bus in his car. When they got there, the children were divvied up among the chaperones, and Scott got a group of five boys. "First we went to the State Capitol, and they learned how the branches of government work. It was fun. I like fooling around with their friends, and, with John, a lot of these kids I had in t-ball and other sports when I was coaching before I got hurt. Actually, all the kids wanted to go with me. I think they just wanted to be able to go in the elevators, instead of up the stairs."

So far so good. Then it was on to the art museum. The groups split up, and Scott took his in and out of exhibition rooms. "And then," he says, "we hit this one room." There on the wall was a bigger-than-life portrait of a naked woman. "One of the kids looked up and said, 'Wow, look at the hair on that thing!' I said, 'Oh my God! OK, that's it, let's get out of here!' Kind of embarrassing, but pretty funny, too. I warned the teacher, 'Better not take the other kids in there!'"

If you can be the alpha dog of a successful Little League team *and* chaperone eleven-year-old boys through a gallery of nudes, then it's possible that you're ready to take on a dance and a date.

In June, Scott's cousin Kim, his Uncle Mike and Aunt Linda's daughter, got married, and all the Remingtons went to the wedding. Gert, especially, loves any event that brings the family together, but she was feeling apprehensive about this one. "I was worried. I didn't know if I wanted to go, because I'm thinking my kids are going to have a great time, they all love to dance, and Scott used to like to dance. And I'm going to be sitting there worrying about him and thinking he's not having fun."

During the reception, though, the DJ made an announcement: Scott Remington was wanted on the dance floor. Scott, who was sitting at a table next to Gert's, leaned over in a mild panic, and said to his mom, "I can't go over there! I can't dance. Who in the world is calling me?" It was his cousin, Shelley Owens—his Uncle Jim and Aunt Cil's eldest daughter—and she just marched over to Scott and dragged him out to the middle of the floor. "Then," Gert laughs, loving the memory, "She just dances with him! She took his hand and swung him around in the wheelchair." Scott returned to his table, but not a few minutes later, a friend of the bride announced that she wanted Scott out there. In full blush, he didn't want to go, but she dragged him out there, and, says Gert, "She sits on his lap! And he wheeled the chair around. You know what? I had the best time. And he had, I think, a better time than anybody."

The dance clearly went well. That August, Scott and Bill Strauss took Kim's friend and a lady-friend of Bill's to Saratoga Springs to see the Dave Matthews Band at the Saratoga Performing Arts Center, a large outdoor venue. What was amazing about that evening was not that, to Bill, Scott was just like he would have been as a teenager, partying and making friends with everyone around them: "It was great, we met some people from Long Island and we talked as if we knew each other." It was what happened when Scott realized he had to pee... real bad.

Scott had had a couple of beers. "I shouldn't've. I know I shouldn't've, but I did it anyway. Y'know, it was the atmosphere and I was having fun, so I had a couple. It's a big amphitheater—about 50,000 people—and we go down through the crowd to where our seats were. They were great, in the third row. And I have to go to the bathroom. You can't feel it like you used to, but you just start to feel full—you have some sensation down there—it's hard to explain. So, shoot, I start to feel like I'm gonna bust. So, I ask a security guard about the bathroom. There's no handicapped bathroom. There were stairs going everywhere. They offered to take me backstage on a stretcher. I said, 'Noooooo! No way.' So, Bill, the girls, and a couple of the guards went with me off to the side and all surrounded me in a circle, and I just catheterized right there. One of the guards held a flashlight for me. He said, 'No problem, people do it here all the time!' Oh God, I was a little embarrassed, needless to say. But Dave Matthews was great. The whole band was great."

To think that this was the guy who had been, at one time, terrified to show his face and his new body in TGI Friday's, or who had broken into a sweat over the prospect of wheeling onto a baseball diamond to tell an eleven-year-old pitcher to arch his back more and follow through. Yet, by that summer, so many people around Scott were shaking their heads in disbelief. Jill Wilson was one: "He's one of a kind, he really is. I mean, some of the things he does! If it's possible to do, he'll do it. If there's ever a chance to walk again, he'll be the first one to do it."

It was that very thought that crossed her mind one summer day, when she walked out onto the beach at her vacation place on Brant Lake. She looked up to see some maniac buzz by on a WaveRunner, signaling with an outstretched arm. "Did I just see Scott go by?" she wondered. "How the hell did he get *there*?"

16.

Onward

It's Friday, March 28, 2003—Scott's fourth fundraiser-eve. Last minute details and anticipation have been building over the past week to fill everyone with a mix of adrenaline and fatigue. But it's good fatigue. With all the lessons from past years and incredible advance work, the committee has every right to be psyched. Shooting to hit the $100,000-in-four-years goal, they hit the pavement hard, pushing advance sales of raffle tickets and taking a shot at some new kinds of publicity. Scott and Ed even appeared on Thursday's morning show on WCKM Radio in Glens Falls. Scott's heart was pounding so hard he was sure you could see it through his shirt, but he and Ed came across cool and relaxed, and John and Jenna were tickled to death. Their school bus driver had turned on the radio so all the kids could hear the interview on their morning ride to school.

By about 2:00 that afternoon, the boxes that had been carefully packed with raffle items and had filled Scott's loft from one end to the other, were loaded into four vehicles, waiting for delivery to Jimbo's early the next morning. It was an impressive sight—thirty-three door prizes, thirty-two kids' items, sixty-five gift certificates, one hundred eleven adult prizes. That's not counting the more than three thousand dollars in checks that folks had already written in direct donations to the Christopher Reeve Paralysis Foundation. By this fundraiser-eve, Scott and Renee were blown away when they tallied $14,000 in pre-event revenue, far eclipsing their record of $8,000 the day before the 2002 event.

Most of the final details fell to Scott, Renee, Wendy, and Gert, who sat around Scott's dining room table, sipping beers and double-checking Renee's meticulous files and the hundreds of labels that had been affixed to plastic lids. Every raffle item would be displayed with its own plastic container whose lid identified the item and donor. Visitors would buy tickets worth one, five, ten, and twenty-five dollars and put them in the containers for the items they hoped to win.

Looking over Renee's list of job assignments, Gert wonders, "Who put Bull on the 50-50? Y'know he'll just visit. He sees someone he knows and he'll be talking instead of selling!"

There are a couple of loose ends, like deciding where they'll post the schedules of events that Renee has printed off her computer. "Let's just put them up by every door," she says, then adds, "Hey, I got it. In the bathrooms! Everybody has to go sometime."

These are all such minor points. For all intents and purposes, they're ready, and it's high time to pack it in, but not before Renee offers Scott one more assurance that there's no need to sweat the weather.

Scott's fundraisers have been blessed with the most uncanny luck as far as weather goes. Even that first year, when the event was set in February, it had been ridiculously warm and clear. Everyone still looks back in awe that a February day in the Adirondacks actually came in at sixty degrees. Go figure. All three previous years, in fact, the event has landed on a day that invited people to spill out of Jimbo's and onto the long porches that look out over Brant Lake to the rear and onto a wide green lawn out front.

It is a fitting end to one of the coldest, snowiest winters in memory that the forecasts for tomorrow are promising a raw, windy day with a nasty rain-snow mix. Scott is beside himself.

"Rain is *good*, Goob," Renee stresses. "We'll probably get a lot of people who would've stayed home to work in their yards. Don't worry about it. Besides which, there's nothing we can do." Scott really, *really* wants to believe her, but it isn't in his nature to relax over anything this close to the benefit.

Renee, Wendy, and Gert pack up the dregs of the day and go home, but only to put on fresh clothes. They will all be meeting in a couple of hours at the town hall.

Their first pre-fundraiser get-together turns out to be everything they hoped it would be. The family brings trays of lasagna, garlic bread, salads, soda, and enough desserts to cover one entire folding table. David Carmel, who is working this year as a White House fellow, is there in a suit, having just flown in from Washington, D.C.; his brother, Jason, is up from his home in New York City to give his presentation on spinal cord research. He could not be speaking to a more appreciative group, and he commands their attention for more than an hour, carefully describing what is happening in the world of neurological research, in a way that is impressive in both scope and detail. Joining the committee members are nearly a dozen disabled residents and their families from the surrounding area. And Scott is especially touched that Mary Vining, director of annual giving for the Christopher Reeve Paralysis Foundation, is up from New Jersey to speak at the fundraiser, and has accepted his invitation to come a day early for the dinner and presentation. What's more, she arrived with Julie Kwon, the foundation's associate director of communications.

Sure enough, Saturday breaks gray and overcast. By 8:00, Jimbo's is buzzing. Joining the core committee is a band of additional friends and relatives who come every year to work the day. Banging and talking echo through the cavernous dining room as tables are being moved, raffle items are being arrayed, band equipment is moving in, and Renee is fielding a thousand questions and problem-solving scores of logistical issues. Scott is wheeling here and there, circulating through the room. "This is total chaos," he worries to a friend, while, a few feet away, Renee is marveling, "This is amazing, we've *never* been this organized."

When the huge room is set with the hundreds of prizes neatly displayed and all the boxes and tape and files are put away, it's show time, and there's still an hour and a half to spare. "We've never had this before," Renee beams. "You wouldn't have believed that first year. We had no clue what we were doing. This is everything we've learned along the way."

Just then, Gert whispers, "I'm not gonna say anything, but look outside." A ray of sunshine has burned through the ominous cloud cover. "The Good Lord knows what we're trying to do here today," she smiles. "Y'know it's not just fun. It's important."

Unfortunately, the beam is a tease. Or maybe it is, indeed, a last-minute, pre-fundraiser salute from Gert's Good Lord. Just about 1:00, as people begin to arrive, the day makes good on the forecasts. A steady, cold rain begins to fall and will continue on-and-off all day and into the evening.

By 1:10, there's already an impressive crowd, but Scott isn't satisfied until, over the course of the next couple of hours, there are, for the fourth year in a row, well over 500 people partying at Jimbo's. Greeting them just inside the main doors are members of the committee and a framed collage that Renee has crafted featuring a picture of Christopher and Dana Reeve, a letter of thanks to Scott from the foundation, and a *New York Times* article on Christopher Reeve's physical therapy breakthroughs.

The crowd moves to the 60s rock, folk, pop, and kick-ass bluegrass. They load the canisters with tickets, hoping to win the 50-50 raffle and hundreds of donated items—everything from gift certificates for gasoline, rafting trips, and restaurants to sweatshirts, jackets, gift baskets, Yankees baseball tickets, automotive supplies, a weed whacker, toys, a red-handled hunting knife with "Spinal Cure 2003" hand-carved into the blade, and a party with Harold Meade & His Smoker. Harold's flyer reads: "Have your favorite meat smoked by me @ your party!! Imagine the possibilities… It's awesome!! I'll supply the smoke & labor. You supply the party. Up to 100 people."

There's a big, soft recliner, too, beside a wooden entertainment center. "No need to sit in that recliner," Scott calls over to Gert, who's testing it out. "You can just deliver it to my house."

"This one's mine," she shoots back. "I'm selling my tickets right from here. Anyone who wants me, this is where I'll be." She ends up putting eighty dollars worth of tickets into the recliner canister, hoping to tip the odds big-time in her favor. At the end of the night, though, Gert will shake her head, disbelieving that her own daughter, Denise, will be going home with that chair after investing one measly ticket.

And for the fourth year in a row, a very special chainsaw sits inconspicuously on the five-dollar-ticket table. The tag reads: "Jonsered Turbo 2165 Chainsaw. Donated by: Anonymous Donors." For the first fundraiser, when Scott's physical and psychic wounds were still so fresh, a group of his friends and relatives had secretly pooled their resources and purchased a chainsaw for the raffle—an anonymous gesture made in homage to Scott and his life as a logger. Scott somehow got wind of it one year, so it's no longer secret, but that doesn't matter. The purchase is now a tradition from the heart—many hearts—and every year "the group" makes sure that there's a brand new chainsaw included among the array of prizes. Even the dealer—who lets them have it for cost—chips in.

Toward early evening, Renee takes the microphone and quiets the festivities to welcome and thank everyone who came and make sure they know that they are all part of the mission to reach the goal of $100,000 in four years.

Around 5:00, Mary Vining introduces the foundation's video, *We Must. We Can. We Will.* Then she speaks to the crowd about the promise of spinal cord research. She thanks everyone profusely for the incredible support, and tells them that everyone at the foundation considers Scott, Renee, their friends and family, and all of the people who have supported them year after year to be part of the foundation family.

Then David Carmel offers an elegant call to action. He invites the crowd to join him in "taking research to the next level" for him, for Scott, and for the hundreds of thousands of others living with spinal cord injury. He urges everyone to write to their New York state legislators asking them to support a bill to permit stem cell research. Then, as an example of what individuals can accomplish when they work together, David surprises Renee, Scott, and everyone else when he introduces a man named Paul Richter who is in the crowd. Paul is a former New York state trooper who was shot while making a traffic stop in 1973. He and his friends lobbied the state legislature for years and eventually won passage of a bill that adds a surcharge to traffic violations and directs the funds to spinal cord research.

"I'll be writing letters night and day," David tells the crowd. "It takes a personal story. It takes constituents to get things done. That and with the money you've raised, we'll take research to the next level. Join with me in the next wave!"

Standing off to the side, listening to Mary welcome everyone into the Christopher Reeve family and hearing David's impassioned remarks, Renee and Wendy start to cry. "We just can't help it," says Renee. "All of this is just the beginning. What David said is right, it's time to move forward. We'll always do this fundraiser, but it's time for us to do some lobbying, or maybe we could have a petition at the door for people to sign. Can you imagine, at the end of one of our fundraisers, having a letter with five hundred signatures to send to the legislature in support of a bill that will help research? That's really what's going to make a difference. This is the beginning, I believe that. So much good has come out of all this. There's so much more we can do."

With every passing hour, Scott gets higher and higher. He's in constant motion and, as he cruises the room, his wheels can't make two revolutions before someone lays a hand on his shoulder, bends down to plant a kiss, stops him to chat, or gives him a high-five. He is the host of this party, and he is dead serious about that responsibility. "My goal is to thank everybody I see," he says. "I'm just so grateful they come out. And they say, 'No problem, we'll be here next year.'" Adding to the day, WCKM Radio, which is running a live broadcast from the benefit, corners him for an interview, and during the raffle he even scores a couple of prizes.

At one point, Renee is watching him off in the distance working the room. "Do you believe him? Look at him. He glows. He's so happy. Mom and I keep telling him he should do some speeches, he'd be great talking to high school kids. He'd be such an inspiration. He says, 'Nah, nah,' but he doesn't know how good he'd be."

The raffles and speeches end sometime after 7:00, and most people call it a night. Soon, though, there are about thirty to forty people hanging out, cleaning off tables, throwing trash in bins, and helping to carry out band equipment. Their kids are helping and running around.

Then a DJ walks to the band area and sets up, and someone dims the lights. It's the end of a long, long day, and committee members have been in motion for nearly twelve hours, but it's not time yet to sleep, not by a long shot. It's time for this hardcore few to get down.

Renee walks over to the bar and Nick—of Nickarita fame—pours her the beer she's been dying for all day. Scott, who's chewed the same piece of gum nearly the whole day, careful not to eat or drink more than a pinch, also knows he's earned a beer… or a few. At the end of this night, he'll let someone drive him home; there are one or two chances that this wildman no longer takes. "The DJ is for us," says Renee. "We started this last year, and it was great. Welcome to the *after* party."

Till almost midnight, they party to celebrate a flawless day. Everyone should be exhausted, but there's little interest in the slow dances. As the rock gets harder, this party gets hotter. Scott gets dragged into a conga line that snakes around the room to an R&B rendition of "Locomotion," and soon after, he's doing a mean air guitar on the dance floor as he and Jenna shake it to "Walk This Way."

Sometime after 10:00, in a rare moment of solitude, Scott is sitting by himself, nodding to the music, watching the show as his favorite people in the world are belting out "Paradise by the Dashboard Light" on the dance floor. A friend walks up and leans down so he can hear over the din: "You did good today, Goob." He looks up and flashes a killer smile.

Sunday dawns an even uglier day. It may be March 30th, but the front that's been locked over the Northeast region is now covering the Adirondacks in snow. To the committee, though, it couldn't be sunnier. Based on a quick tally of the revenues in hand—from the raffles, cash donations to Christopher Reeve, food and beer sales, and the more than six hundred dollars that the 50-50 winner turned around and gave back to the committee—after all expenses are paid, the 2003 Scott Remington Family & Close Friends Spinal Cord Research Benefit has netted $30,880. Over the next few weeks, even more checks will roll in from businesses, friends, and folks who couldn't make it to the fundraiser or saw a flyer or heard Scott and Ed on the radio. The $100,000 goal is more than theirs.

The end of each fundraiser is a natural time to take stock. In the calm after the day, as everyone is assessing the event and making mental notes of new lessons learned for next year, Scott can't help looking back. It's hard to process the generosity and goodwill that keeps pouring from his community, just as it gets tougher, not easier, to make sense of what's become of his life over the past four years. He's lived it, and it's still hard to believe.

It's just so hard for him to get his hands around the fact that so much good has come from the worst experience he could possibly imagine. How did it happen that a trip to hell gave him the chance to witness the heights of human kindness, and to discover that his own strength and sense of caring reach farther and deeper than he ever knew? How can his life feel so full, when he still grieves over how much he's lost?

It's weird when he thinks that he might actually be able to handle talking to some groups, maybe high school students. He survived the radio interview, didn't he? And earlier in March, after reluctantly agreeing to talk to his niece Dakota's second grade class about living in a wheelchair, he couldn't believe how nervous he had been when he started and how pumped he felt when he finished.

He's also thinking that he should take David up on his invitation to get involved in the politics of the battle for a cure. Now *that* would be something. Imagine him writing letters to legislators and maybe traveling down to Albany for a public hearing.

Could life be more surreal? Four years after his accident, he's still adjusting to life in a body that he wasn't born in, didn't go to school in, and didn't get married in. Like Wendy says, there's still a tear a day. But then you figure that, over those same four years, a movie star sent him a personal, videotaped message, and he sent the movie star more than $100,000. There's only one explanation for every minute of every day since May 25, 1999. It was all just an accident.

Afterthoughts

It seems to be a human reflex to try to make sense of tragedy. The more shocking and random the tragedy, the more driven we are to try to figure it out. That "figuring out" is a key step in the coping process, and it appears to center on two questions: How could this happen? and What do we do now?

Scott's family perfectly shows that the first question is an entirely personal struggle. Even members of the same close-knit group can take very different routes to the answer, and some never get to an answer at all.

In the remarkable journal that Scott's family kept for him, which included the entries during his time in the ICU, as well as many others through all his dark days in the hospital, his mother repeatedly urged him to find strength in faith. She cited chapter and verse from biblical texts—Matthew, Peter, Romans, Nehemiah, Philippians, Thessalonians, Hebrews, Psalms. She was clearly hanging on for dear life to the words of comfort and encouragement that she found in her Bible and heard from her pastor, continually reminding Scott that every baby step forward was evidence that God was with him. The Lord, she constantly reminded him, would be his rock and his light to the end of the tunnel. *He* was her rock and her light as well.

Religious devotion and spirituality, though, don't always make the coping process easier. Sometimes they make it harder. Plenty of people of great faith have been stopped in their tracks by tragedy, wondering how He could *ever* let this happen. In the face of tragedy, religion stops being their rock, and, instead, turns to sponge—no longer a source of certainty, it is suddenly porous. The problem is that so many tragedies simply defy logic, and so they challenge faith-inspired explanations that have seemed so right and so comforting in other situations.

More than three years after Scott's accident, his dear friend and brother-in-law, John Smith, still couldn't stop turning it all over in his mind. The serendipity of it all haunts him. "I don't wish this upon anybody," he said. "I still have this question—here's a man who went to work, and he's providing for his family, and it changes in an instant. I know things happen for a reason, but I've tried, and I don't know why this happened. I probably will never know."

Then there are others whose pragmatic outlooks on life just accept that nature can produce a confluence of factors that lead a man into the exact trajectory of a falling tree limb. For instance, it worries Scott's family to no end that Denise's husband, Bill, continues to work in the woods alone. The way Bill sees it, though, he always has, always will. He's been a logger all his life, since age five in fact (but that's another story), and he's "seen a lot." What he's seen is that, "A lot of the accidents in this field could be prevented. That's why I say I prefer to work by myself, because I have found over the years I get hurt a lot less than most other people. I know everything that's going on around me."

Then again, he concedes, no one could have prevented what happened to Scott. "Some things," he says with perfect calm and clarity, "are just accidents."

So the route to "How could this happen?" can be a varied one indeed—beginning and ending in different places depending on who we are and the emotional baggage that we carry.

But when it comes to "What now?" the Remingtons, along with all of their extended family, friends, and neighbors, without consulting each other or even realizing it, embarked on the same route and arrived at the same conclusion.

It's a conclusion that can be explained with uncanny precision by an ancient anecdote. It's a simple pearl of wisdom that can appeal to any of us, no matter what religion we identify with or whether we have any religion at all. We don't even have to believe in God or consider ourselves the least bit spiritual.

It's been said that, in ancient times, when the Israelites fled Pharaoh's Egypt, they set up tents in the desert for worship. The tents were supported by wooden poles, and the sockets where those supporting poles met—those points of connection—were called *adanim*. It turns out that the word, *adanim*, shares the same three root sounds as the word *Adonai*, one of the Hebrew names for God.

Some sages interpreted this linguistic coincidence by suggesting that *adanim* was actually a key to the meaning of *Adonai*. That is, they posited, God is the master of making connections, or, put another way, God is the one who helps me to master making connections.

If you enjoy wrestling ideas at all, this is as good as it gets.

Consider that, in any language, in any country or culture on earth, and at any time in the history of the world, our ability to make peace or progress, our ability to triumph over the most challenging obstacles, our success in feeling happy or fulfilled, often boils down to one thing—our ability to form connections. From the international to the cellular level, we humans need to connect—reaching out to others, letting them reach in to us, cooperating, understanding… just connecting.

In other words, this little linguistic intersection might actually suggest what "It" is all about. Maybe life is, in large part, about embracing a "higher" power, but not necessarily one that you'll find by casting your eyes upward, because it is grounded here on earth. It's a power that is inherent in every organism and in all of us.

When life seems to be coming apart at the seams – from a death, failed relationship, tragic accident, conflict, disappointment—it's uncanny how often the pain and torment of those experiences can be traced to an *adanim* breakdown, a rupture or loss of connections. And our efforts to recover almost always involve forming new connections or finding solace and new energy in our surviving connections.

In Scott's case, the idea of ruptured connections was present in all of its figurative and literal senses. His rescue from death and despair, his recovery and renewal had everything to do with reconnecting, from the physical reparations and reconnections that his doctors performed to the emotional ones that his friends, family, and community performed. Scott can take a lot of credit for his own salvation. He also owes an incalculable debt to those who refused to let him fall—those who stitched his body back together, and those who constructed an emotional scaffold that sustained him through both the loss of his legs and the loss of his marriage.

Something that Ellen McDermott said about her friend, Renee, could have been said of any number of friends and loved ones who rallied around him. "I never dreamed he'd recuperate the way he did," she said. "I really have to give a lot of that to Renee. That big sister, she was a little pain in the ass. I mean it. Sometimes, I was like, 'Let up a little bit! Let him wallow for a little while, he deserves it.' And she just would never let him. If I ever needed help, I think I'd want Renee in my corner, because she just never let up. Never."

Substitute any one of a hundred other names, and Ellen's insight holds—Gert, Bull, Earle, Denise and Bill, Steph and Keith, John, Joss, John-Roscoe, Jenna, Chris, Lynn, Jim and Cil, Chris and Ed, the Meades, the Wilsons, Bill Lajeunesse, Bill Strauss, Kenny, Toni, Esther, Barbara, Barb, Gabriella, the list goes on and on.

At no time, from the moment that beech tree fell, did they let up. Every little pain in the ass pitched in to build and reinforce a lifeline that reconnected Scott to the world and never gave way.

And in so doing, by accident, they discovered nothing less than the meaning of life.

Note of Thanks

T alk about accidents. Stumbling onto Scott has been one of my life's most unexpected and happy experiences.

As a freelance writer who primarily supports corporate clients, it's been an inspiration to write for the Christopher Reeve Paralysis Foundation. In 2002, while working on a CRPF publication, *Walking Tomorrow*, I was composing "briefs" about various fundraisers around the country that had sent money to the foundation. Scott was on my list of people to call.

It was supposed to be a quick conversation to get the amount donated and the nature of the event. And in fact, within a few minutes, I had the information I needed about Scott's third fundraiser, but for some reason we kept on talking—for nearly an hour. He was engaging and surprisingly open about his situation and about living with paralysis in general, especially since he didn't know me at all. In the course of our conversation, he asked me about my work, and said that he always wanted to write about his experience, because living with paralysis is a challenge every single day, and he felt he had so much to share.

That night, I told my husband about this surprising conversation I had had with a logger from upstate New York and what Scott said about wanting to write about his experience. Charlie looked at me and said, "You should do this." Just like that.

I obsessed for about a week, until I worked up the nerve to call Scott back. "Remember me?" I said. "I think I'd like to explore the possibility of writing your story. Can I just meet you?"

He said, "C'mon up." Just like that.

We set a date, and I drove up to the Adirondacks. Even though it was a beastly August day, as I got close to Scott's exit, I'm not kidding, I started to feel chills—*Where was I and what the heck was I doing?*

Scott had told me that there was no way I'd find his house on my own, so I should pull into the post office parking lot in Brant Lake, call him on my cell phone, and he'd drive up in his Jeep and lead me to his house. I waited nervously, and finally a Jeep pulled up with the top off and two kids in the back. I smiled and waved. He waved back and motioned for me to follow. At his house, we introduced ourselves and settled into his small basement office for a chat. As I reached into my bag for pad, pen, and tape recorder, my hands were shaking a little. He noticed, smiled, and told me, "Hey, don't be nervous. Nothin' to be nervous about."

Those were the first of so many words of wisdom from Scott. We spent four hours talking that first day about his accident and his life. I went home and thought about it some more, and, still not certain how we were going to pull this off, I called him back and told him, "I'd really like to give this a try. Do you want to go on an adventure with me?"

"Let's go," he said, then added, "Hey, I just thought of something. I've always known how a tree becomes paper, now I get to see paper become a book."

How great is that?

It was fascinating and incredibly fun to work with Scott and get to know his family, his friends, and his world. And it soon became clear to me that Scott did, in fact, have something important to share. His contribution in doing this project and letting me crawl around in his life is "the truth."

If he said it once, he said it a million times, "Ask me anything. Whatever you want to know I'll tell you." He was brave and steadfast in his efforts to communicate what it's like to live in his body. It was not easy for him to tell me the gory details, *really* not easy sometimes, but he refused to give in to his discomfort. He was committed to the process and the goal, and, along the way, he bent over backward to make it as easy as possible for me to ask him what he thinks, what he feels, and how he does everything big and small. "Just tell it, Amy. Just get the emotion, and it will be right," is what he said.

So many times when I'd tell him the names of people I had scheduled to interview, Scott called those people ahead of me, and instructed them to "tell her everything. Tell her the truth." When his friend, Bill Lajeunesse, told

Scott that he'd held off telling me about the time when Scott nearly burned up in his hunting camp, Scott got all over Bill's case. Bill called me back a few days after our interview, and let me know that Scott had instructed him to set the record straight.

Scott worked so hard to make me understand the constant state of extremes that tends to characterize a life that has been touched by catastrophe—how you can be "doing great" but still feel like crap, how you can appear to be so together while you harbor awful doubts, and how so many wonderful things and so much personal growth can come from such an experience, but you'd chuck it all in a heartbeat to get your old self back. He is a tough, fun, physical guy, who never considered himself an intellectual, yet he demonstrated an astounding capacity to be moving, insightful, analytical, and articulate.

Scott's not perfect. He readily admitted to doubts he's had, to reaching his emotional limits, to mistakes he made in his life. He is, however, perfectly honest – as Tom McPhillips put it, a no-holds-barred guy, who's candid to a fault. He is also a joy to know.

I take full responsibility for the quality of this presentation and the accuracy of the content. However, the credit for anything in this account that is compelling, helpful, or eye-opening goes to Scott. He's the one who put his soul on the line.

So many other people were part of the truth squad that made this project possible. I am grateful beyond measure for their knowledge, patience, humor, and candor.

Scott's family accepted me with open arms into the fold. I feel like I've made friends for life. Their warmth and willingness to revisit painful memories were critical in making this account complete. I couldn't have done it without them. This very special bunch includes: John "Bull" and Gert Remington; John "Roscoe" Remington; Jenna Remington; Earle Remington; Renee, John, and Joss-Elyse Smith; Denise and Bill MacGlashan; Stephanie and Keith Wood; Bud DeMatties; Ed and Chris Jay; and Jim and Priscilla Remington.

For the record, Cindy chose not to participate in this project. I respect her decision.

For helping me to understand the science behind Scott's situation and, in some cases, for sharing their personal and professional recollections of and experiences with Scott, I am deeply indebted to: Dr. James H. Barada, Dr. Barbara T. Benevento, Dr. William Brand, Dr. Robert J. D'Agostini, Barbara Garrett, Esther Halden, Susan Howley, Dr. Douglas Landsman, Toni Longshore, Donna Lowich, Tom Ringrose, Mary Sprano, Gabriella Stiefbolt, Sally Vinskus, Dr. Lauren Vocaturo, and Dr. Paul Wangenheim.

Scott's friends and co-workers took me into their confidence and clearly took to heart Scott's directive to tell me everything. For answering all of my questions and happily dishing about Scott, my thanks to: Brent Bullock, Steve Bureau, David Carmel, Roger Daby, Rick Davidson, Nick deGregory, Karl and Ann Dingman, Stacey Dobbs, Jim Farrar, Kenny Higgins, Trish Jarvis-Weber, Bryce Johnson, Chris Johnson, Bill Lajeunesse, Ellen McDermott, Tom and Lois McPhillips, Marty Mead, Ted and Wendy

Meade, Barb Mullaney, David Osterberg, Jim Peck, Johnny Pratte, Joe Rizzi, Ray Saladin, Steve Satterfield, Bill Strauss, and Gary and Jill Wilson.

On my end, when my son, Ben, said, "Mom, I'll be your muse," that was one of my luckiest days. He turned the parent-child table on me, took this business writer under his wing, and gave me insight into things like voice, color, character, point of view, and storytelling. His lessons were beyond value. Also on the home front, Charlie and Henry never doubted me, or, thank goodness, did a great job of faking it.

For inspiration, thank you so much David Wechsler-Azen, bet you never dreamed that one story would reveal for one woman the meaning of life. Maggie Goldberg of the Christopher Reeve Paralysis Foundation, gifted me with extremely honest insights, encouragement, and, especially, friendship. My friend, Will Hubscher, took me out on therapy lunches and boosted me from day one. Marilyn Jones, who created the cover of this book, proved once again that artists really do see the world through special eyes. Bill and Kris Tribou were ready at a moment's notice with food, shelter, warmth, and support. Trish and Eric Weber were wonderful for indulging my whims and spending a day in the Adirondack woods that I'll never forget. Pat Reilly-Hovey, confidante and running mate, let me unload over so many miles. Mary Liz McNamara and Rick Schlosser read my first draft and made me feel like I was onto something. (Just knowing Mary Liz is a constant reminder that it's never too late to try.) Tracie, Kris, Cheryl, and AQ at AuthorHouse, thanks for taking great care of me.

And Mr. Christopher Reeve, you changed our definition of "possible," because you refused to sit still. Your ripple effect will last forever.

About The Author

Amy Montgomery is a New Jersey-based freelance writer, who has worked primarily with corporate clients across a range of industries. She has also worked as a radio reporter, press secretary, and adjunct instructor at the University of Michigan. She has a BA from Wesleyan University and an MA from the University of Michigan.

Printed in the United States
25498LVS00001B/33

9 781418 492908